"They spent much of the 33 months between their arrest and conviction in solitary confinement. This contempt for human rights is unworthy of a democratic country. I urge that these men be returned to their homes and lives in Cuba."
—Nadine Gordimer, Nobel prizewinner for literature and vice-president of International PEN

"How is it that a government so intent on waging war against terrorism, as it calls it, is itself involved in protecting terrorists in its own country, who are attacking, and have been attacking for many years, and have caused the deaths of more people in Cuba than died on September 11?" —Ramsey Clark, former U.S. Attorney General

"To fight for the freedom of these noble Cubans is a duty for all the forces that stand against terrorism in any part of the world. It is to struggle for the cause of so many other prisoners who, like them, are condemned to unjust sentences in U.S. prisons, and who we cannot forget." —Angela Davis

"The five Cubans who have been imprisoned in the United States remain a secret from the people of the United States. That story does not appear in the American press. You hear nothing about it... It's totally in violation not just of constitutional rights, but of human rights." —Howard Zinn

"If a political prisoner can be defined as one kept in custody who, if not for his or her political beliefs and/or associations would be a free person, then the five Cubans can be regarded as political prisoners." —William Blum

"For well over four decades, the U.S. empire has been waging a secret and deadly war against Cuba. They have bombed fields, poisoned grain, hijacked planes and plotted invasions. They have trained, paid and protected terrorists who have cost the lives of thousands of Cubans, and virtually crippled their economy through a seemingly everlasting embargo.

"The Cuban Five, young men who tried to protect their people from these instances of U.S. state terrorism; who bombed no one — nor planned to; who poisoned no one — nor planned to; who hurt no one; who merely reported the plotting of crimes against their people, faced the full, foul fury of the empire's judiciary — for trying to stop the crimes!" — Mumia Abu-Jamal

"The thing with the Cuban Five is such a scandal." — Noam Chomsky

"These five heroic Cubans are being punished precisely because of the fact that they truly did fight against terrorism, even at the cost of their own lives. Those who have taken away their freedom and sought to slander and denigrate them have done so because they dared to combat the heinous criminals who were created and continue to be protected by those very same authorities. Every hour they spend locked up in that living hell is an insult to the memory of those who lost their lives on September 11 and to all other victims of terrorism. It is also an affront to all those who believe in dignity and human decency."

— Ricardo Alarcón, president of the National Assembly of Cuba

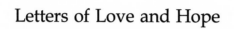
Letters of Love and Hope

Letters of Love and Hope

The Story of the Cuban Five

Alice Walker
Nancy Morejón
The Families of the Cuban Five
Leonard I. Weinglass

René González Sehwerert
Antonio Guerrero Rodríguez
Fernando González Llort
Ramón Labañino Salazar
Gerardo Hernández Nordelo

Ocean Press
Melbourne ■ New York
www.oceanbooks.com.au

Cover design by ::maybe

ISBN 10: 1-920888-23-3
ISBN 13: 978-1-920888-23-7
Library of Congress Catalog Card No: 2005921480
First Printed 2005
Printed in Canada

PUBLISHED BY OCEAN PRESS

Australia: GPO Box 3279, Melbourne, Victoria 3001, Australia
           Fax: (61-3) 9329 5040 Tel: (61-3) 9326 4280
           E-mail: info@oceanbooks.com.au
USA: PO Box 1186, Old Chelsea Stn., New York, NY 10113-1186, USA
           Tel: (1-212) 260 3690

OCEAN PRESS DISTRIBUTORS

United States and Canada: **Consortium Book Sales and Distribution**
           Tel: 1-800-283-3572   www.cbsd.com
Australia and New Zealand: **Palgrave Macmillan**
           E-mail: customer.service@macmillan.com.au
UK and Europe: **Pluto Books**
           E-mail: pluto@plutobooks.com
Cuba and Latin America: **Ocean Press**
           E-mail: oceanhav@enet.cu

www.oceanbooks.com.au
info@oceanbooks.com.au

My love, suppose that I go far away
so far that I forget my name.
My love, perhaps I am a different man
taller and younger, waiting for himself
far away, over there, climbing up the sweet abyss.

My love, suppose there is no way out
when that is all I seek.
My love, take this thought
place it at the center of all selfishness
and see that the sweet abyss is never absent.

My love, suppose that in forgetting
the night leaves me prisoner.
My love, there will be a bright new star
of light and hope that will not be extinguished,
endless potential concealed beneath the sweet abyss.

My love, brightness envelops me,
I will leave and you will keep our garden.
My love, I will return, awake,
for another stubborn morning of music and poetry,
I will return from the sun that illuminates the sweet abyss.

Silvio Rodríguez
"The Sweet Abyss"

Contents

Editorial Note

In September 1998, five Cubans living in Miami were arrested and charged with conspiracy to commit espionage and conspiracy to commit murder. The "crime" of these Cubans was to monitor terrorist groups in Florida that have acted — and continue to act — with impunity from U.S. territory against an independent and sovereign country, the nearby island of Cuba. Ironically, in the wake of the events of September 11, on December 2001 they were sentenced to appallingly long terms of imprisonment. The five Cubans, René González Sehwerert, Antonio Guerrero Rodríguez, Fernando González Llort, Ramón Labañino Salazar and Gerardo Hernández Nordelo have been labelled as spies, but their trials alone indicate the political nature of their imprisonment.

This book contains correspondence spanning five years between these Cuban prisoners and their families, allowing the reader a glimpse of how ordinary families cope in extraordinary circumstances. Along with essays by the renowned U.S. writer Alice Walker and Cuban poet Nancy Morejón, *Letters of Love and Hope* also includes a succinct legal analysis of the case by attorney Leonard Weinglass, outlining both its background and its significant violations of both international law and the U.S. constitution.

René González Sehwerert, one of the five Cubans who were all convicted in U.S. courts of justice, spoke the following words in his defense at trial:

> People here have spoken with impunity against Cuba, censuring a nation of people whose only crime is having chosen their

own path, and having defended that choice successfully, at the cost of enormous sacrifices...

When Mr. Kastrenakas [lawyer for the prosecution] stood up in this courtroom, this symbol of U.S. justice, and said we had come here to destroy the United States, he showed how little that symbol and that justice matter to him...

The evidence in this case, history, our beliefs — none of this supports the absurd idea that Cuba wants to destroy the United States. The problems of the human race cannot be resolved by destroying any country — for too many centuries, empires have been destroyed only for similar or worse empires to be built on their ruins. Threats to this nation will not come from a people like the people of Cuba, where it is considered immoral to burn a flag, whether it is from the United States or any other country.

With the privilege of having been born here and of growing up in Cuba, I would like to tell the people of the United States not to look so far to the south to see the threat to the United States.

Cling to the real and genuine values that inspired the founding fathers of this nation. The lack of these values, sidelined by less idealistic interests, constitute the real threat to this society. Power and technology can become weaknesses if they are not in the hands of a cultured people, and the hatred and ignorance we have seen here toward a small country, that nobody knows, can be dangerous when combined with a blinding sense of power and false superiority.

Go back to Mark Twain and forget about Rambo if you really want to leave your children a better country. Every alleged Christian who was brought up to this courtroom to lie, after swearing on the Bible, is a threat to this country, in view of the way their conduct serves to undermine these values.

The editors
February 2005

Alice Walker*
The Story of the Cuban Five

Now that you are with me
My people and the dignity of the world.
— Ramón Labañino Salazar

The story of the Cuban Five is one of courage, great sacrifice and love. It is a story for the ages; especially for those of our people who have suffered under the implacable oppression of white American supremacy, a rule of color and power the rest of the world appears destined to experience. In September 1998 five Cuban men, Gerardo Hernández Nordelo, Ramón Labañino Salazar, Antonio Guerrero Rodríguez, Fernando González Llort and René González Sehwerert, were arrested in the state of Florida. Charged with espionage and other "crimes" against the United States, they were convicted in Miami, a place notorious for its hatred of the Cuban Revolution, Fidel Castro and all things relevant to the social, cultural and spiritual aspirations of the Cuban people. The five men were treated atrociously, as Cubans routinely have been — darker-skinned Cubans even more so — in prisons in the United States. Although judges were unable to define a specific "crime" the Five had committed, beyond attempting to discover and alert their country of planned

---

*Alice Walker has received numerous awards for her fiction, nonfiction and poetry, including the Pulitzer prize in 1983 for *The Color Purple*.

terrorist attacks — which Cuba has suffered for decades from Miami-based Cubans supported by the U.S. government — they were treated sadistically. Denied bail, separated from their families and kept for 17 months in solitary confinement in an attempt to break their bodies and their spirits. They were given ridiculously long sentences: one of them, Gerardo Hernández Nordelo, was given two life sentences plus 15 years. And there are other horrors that the men in these pages refrain from describing out of compassion for their families and the people of Cuba who suffer intensely from their plight.

The treatment they have received is shameful; the silence around this treatment even more so. Where are the congress members, the senators and representatives we should be able to rely on in cases like this? People with the courage to insist that prisoners not be subjected to torture. That their children not be denied access to them; that their wives and mothers not be driven to despair by the many failed attempts they make to see their wrongly, in this case, incarcerated kin. Unfortunately, many of our leaders seem to view Florida's Cuban conservatives, including the assassins and terrorists among them, as People Who Vote. It appears they will endure any degree of inhumanity against any number of babies, children, old grandaunts and nursing mothers, grandfathers and soccer players, if they can secure the collective vote from this terrifying electorate.

Fortunately, my introduction to this slim volume is not about the painful failings of our leaders, who never seem to realize how we, who vote for them, also suffer when they do nothing while good people (like the Cuban Five, whose behavior we can completely understand), are crucified for trying to prevent destruction of human life.

What floated up to consciousness for me as I read these letters back and forth between incarcerated fathers, sons, husbands, and their wives, children and mothers, attempting desperately to reconnect, was a realization of how old this story really is. When I read these letters and poems and viewed the drawings, I was connected to those of our ancestors who first experienced the wrenching devastation of the destruction of their families. I felt in my own body the long centuries of slavery, the systematic — and to our ancestors, insane — focus of the slave owners on tearing families apart. How courageously so many of our ancestors must have defended, or tried to defend, this precious unit, the family. How many centuries it must have taken to almost conquer familial devotion. For some of our ancestors the voiding of familial feeling was achieved. They became zombies who learned to help their masters subdue and destroy others who were enslaved. Their descendents are those today who sell, within as well as outside their families of birth, crack cocaine and other addictive drugs. They are also the allies of those in power, aiding and abetting the squashing of all rebellious, "disobedient" life.

There are fathers in the hundreds of thousands in jail in the United States, and a huge number of mothers as well. What is happening to their children, who frequently follow their parents into a lifetime of encounters with police enforcement, humiliation, loss of contact with society, incarceration? How defenseless these children are, and how robbed of the love and guidance that should be every child's birthright.

When I was asked to write an introduction to this book I had no idea how it would speak to me. I was attending the 2004 International Book Fair in Havana; my own book *Meridian* had been translated into Spanish and was being presented. I flew in for the occasion and found that Cuba now has a 100 percent literacy rate. It was amazing to see the hundreds of children, mothers, fathers, grandparents — everyone it seemed — rushing to the book fair on foot. The fair itself was held in what used to be a fort. The room in which my book was presented and, afterward, a dialogue convened, was just behind what had been, during his lifetime, the office of Che Guevara. A bronze bust of him graces the foyer. As I was being interviewed I stroked his metal locks, amused, as I think he would have been, that so fluid a spirit had been memorialized in such a monument. To me, Che continues to have a luminosity, a radiance, meaning, I think, that he will be remembered, and used as a guide, for many generations to come. His example of how to live and die must certainly be part of the nourishment that sustains Los Cinco, as the Cuban Five are affectionately called.

As determined as they were to bring Elián González home, that is how determined every Cuban I spoke with seemed to be on freeing the Cuban Five. Not a single conversation failed to end on their situation, even if it started someplace else. It was Ricardo Alarcón, president of the National Assembly of Cuba, who talked to me about the letters and drawings that had been made into a book and asked if I would consider introducing it. Although I support the Cuban Revolution because I also believe in free education, health care, 100 percent literacy and the other goals and accomplishments it has achieved, I am by nature wary of leaders. Even modest, excellent ones, as Alarcón has the reputation of being. Too many disappointments. And so I was not, at the moment of being asked, overjoyed, though I was deeply impressed by the intensity of everyone's appreciation of the Five. Los Cinco are heroes to their people of the kind usually encountered in myth.

However, as I started reading, I began to see how important this book is for our time. *The time of so many parents in prison.* It is a primer that can be put to use immediately for the teaching of one of the most important lessons of all: how to be a father, how to be a husband, how to be a lover, *how to parent,* when something as large and compassionless as the U.S. government stands between you and everything you love.

By the time I was arrested, on September 12, 1998, you were barely four and a half months old. The night before, your mommy had gone to work and I was taking care of you. When I finished giving you your milk you fell asleep on me and I decided to leave you there while I watched television. When your mommy arrived, she thought you were so cute sleeping like that — sprawled over me looking contented — so she couldn't resist taking a picture of us. That's the last one where we're together.

Then they arrested me and I could not even kiss you good-bye. When they were taking me out of the house handcuffed, all I could do was look at your mommy and give her a smile, confident and optimistic. (*René González*)

It is this smile, "confident and optimistic," that the men struggle to beam — from prisons situated in five separate locations in the United States — over the heads of their children, as the distance grows and years pass. It is a warmth, a passion, a love, extremely moving to witness. It says something basic, I believe, about the human heart. "Until our hearts are completely vanquished, our children will continue to hear from us." No doubt there will be times when the children of these men complain that, because their fathers were not physically with them while they were growing up, they are delinquent, irres-ponsible parents. And yet, because these few, precious documents exist these same children will have evidence that, though out of their fathers' presence, they were never out of their fathers' love. To be a revolutionary means, by definition, to be willing to sacrifice. One's comfort, one's joy, one's health and life if necessary. But what child wants to be part of a sacrifice? What child can understand the absence of a parent who — in trying to save the lives of all the citizens of one's country — is missing from the birthday party given when one is 10?

When we were able to see each other again you were one year old, eight months had passed. We were under surveillance and when you realized that I was handcuffed to the chair you must have thought I was a dog because you started saying "bow-wow, bow-wow." Then your mommy tried to make you see what was really happening. "No, Ivette" she told you, her indignant expression sarcastic, "your daddy isn't the dog here." In spite of the conditions, we remained in good spirits during the visit.

(*René González*)

These people, these Cubans, demonized for so long because stubbornly they choose their own way, are simply people, simply human beings. It should not be necessary to destroy them to make their country safe for McDonald's and Starbucks.

The Cuban love of education mirrors the passion with which African Americans have traditionally viewed knowledge and learning. My own parents, some of the poorest people in the United States, with almost no resources beyond their determination, built the first school for black children in my community. It was immediately burned to the ground by white landowners. Incredibly, they, like the Cubans, were not swayed from their course, but managed, somehow, to erect another school. Every time I think of this, and of the 40 million functionally illiterate people in the United States, I wish with all my heart that North Americans had had the good fortune to have people like my own parents leading the country. What a different place it would be.

It's my role as a father to be up-to-date and always to be teaching — even at a distance. So I'm sending a drawing to Lizbeth, my little one who can't read yet, with some ideas and tasks for you to read to her. I'd like you to hang this drawing over her bed: it's meant to be a serious duckling, questioning whether she's done her daily chores (the list underneath). That way, she'll always see it, so that she'll remember her daddy and at the same time remember her daily responsibilities, and the drawings and notes will give her encouragement. (*Ramón Labañino*)

My dearest son, Gabriel Eduardo,

I don't know when your mother will give you this letter — she'll know to pick the best time. There's a reason why I haven't been able to see you for so many years. I hope that you'll forgive me for not telling you sooner, but you were too little to explain things to... My hope is for you to grow up to be a good person, useful to society, loyal to a true and worthy cause. Thus, you'll need to study hard, since knowledge will help you to understand and shape the world around you. The most important thing is that you be a generous person, since individualism and egotism aren't worth a thing. "The person who gives of himself grows." As Che said to his children: "Above all, always be capable of feeling deeply any injustice committed against anyone, anywhere in the world." Be honest, just, brave, and you'll always be respected. Love your country, Panama, and your people... (*Antonio Guerrero*)

This is a book whose beauty sinks in slowly, as the reader gradually comprehends the seriousness of what is being attempted. Nothing less than being fully present to the growth of one's children while being not only absent but locked up, far away, in a small prison cell. In a place where there is ice and snow.

My beloved little daughters,

...Now you can understand why daddy couldn't be with you longer, or share all the happy times with you like other fathers do with their children. For that, I'm very sorry.

For that, and for my absences, because I couldn't be at mommy's side during her pregnancy, because I couldn't see you be born, because I couldn't be there when you opened your precious eyes for the first time, or to change your diapers, or help you to take your first steps or clean up your "pee-pee" and "poo," or see your first smiles or hear your first words — the first "daddy," "mommy" or "I love you." For not taking care of you when you were sick or playing with you all the games fathers love to play with their children, not even being able to teach you your first vowels or read you your first book, and for the fact that my littlest one barely knows me. For all that, I apologize, my beloved daughters.

But I want you to know that I had to leave because of my love for you and everyone. That wherever I have been and wherever I will be, you have been and will always be with me.

Be strong, very strong to face whatever life brings with a smile. Don't be afraid for me, I am well and I am strong, especially now that you are with me like my people and the dignity of the world. I'll come back, never doubt that, as soon as I can, because I miss you very much. When I come home, we'll make up for all my absences, and rebuild all the hopes and dreams that have been waiting for us... (*Ramón Labañino*)

Like our own beloved Mumia Abu-Jamal, likewise innocent, likewise framed, also a hero by any standard — locked down on death row for so many pitiless years — these men are demonstrating something extraordinary that must not be missed by the rest of us: that continuing to love with depth and tenderness honors revolution at its highest success.

Alice Walker
Mendocino, California, July 21, 2004

Nancy Morejón*
The Cuban Five: A Remarkable Family Story

After reading this fusion of letters, diary entries, poems, drawings
and personal thoughts by the wives and children of the five Cubans
so unjustly imprisoned in the United States, the truth emerges of a
story in which the key elements have been distorted and, worse,
deceitfully silenced.

Whoever reads these pages, which break this silence, will be able
to reconstruct the most important series of events for René González,
Antonio Guerrero, Fernando González, Ramón Labañino and Gerardo Hernández since September 12, 1998 (the date they were arrested).
They will also be able to learn the hidden side to those events, to
cross the threshold of an incredible fortress of feelings. That fortress
is in reality a vast edifice built on the foundations of dignified sacrifice and profound moral values, which are so pure they are both
beautiful and deeply moving. The roof of the fortress, its walls and
windows, give us a lesson in hope and love, in resistance and gener-
osity, rarely seen in episodes of such political importance and such
pathos.

---

*Nancy Morejón is the best known and most widely translated woman
poet of post-revolutionary Cuba and regularly tours the United States.
Her work addresses contemporary issues of ethnicity, gender, history,
politics and Afro-Cuban identity.

This is real history, woven by the fine, firm, kind and brave hands of its first targets, its first to suffer: the mothers, the wives, the closest friends and the children of these five Cubans — whether they were born here or over there. Their integrity of purpose and their shining shields have only one source of sustenance: the homeland, but in the sense meant by José Martí, the universal Cuban and poet of *The Golden Age*, when he said: "Our homeland is humanity."

Like the vast number of Cubans today, whose intellectual force is without precedent, we watch these men overcome adversity through literature, not only in reading, but also in writing — one of the most impressive ways to improve life on this amazing, infinite planet. From their iniquitous prison cells, these five men teach us the vital necessity of reading and of ennobling and enlightening hobbies such as learning how to grow bonsai; how to appreciate animals; how to discover the hidden knowledge of stamp collecting — the process of learning through collecting stamps from other latitudes. This is their special way of defending their right to dream, to rid themselves of the spiritual impoverishment that — in spite of all available technological developments — afflicts this heart-breaking beginning of a new century and a new millennium.

The poetry in these texts was not born from imported ideals but from the very hand of each author. It was not born of vanity or from a desire to proselytize or a need to be didactic. Nor was it born from any literary ambition — although that would be perfectly legitimate under the circumstances — but from the integral ethics of a fugitive and untamable ancestral spirit. This poetry comes from life itself, from the need for a complete existence, from the desire for healthier relations between men and women, beyond biological procreation.

Radiantly co-existing in this marvelous spiral is the indestructible, exceptional institution of the Cuban family, along with a love for a homeland that for over four decades has faced the most hostile isolation without losing its humanist vocation. The daily landscape inhabited by these women and children is imbued with a dignity that is supported by tenderness and integrity. Alongside the transparent innocence of the children, so full of grace and humor, there circulates in these pages the soul of a nation that is articulated and defended by simple, everyday anecdotes or through drawings that are strongly reminiscent of the brilliance of Saint-Exupéry's *The Little Prince*.

This battle is being waged not only for the image and dignity of Cuba, but for that of the universe. With human beings like Olga, Mirta, Rosa, Elizabeth and Adriana, not just a better island but a better world is more than possible.

Nancy Morejón
Havana, April 4, 2004

The Families of the Cuban Five
Simple, Elemental Justice

We have managed to put this book together using our memories, our grief and our hopes. We have reviewed one by one the letters of our sons and husbands, we have removed photographs from their frames, we have cried and laughed while reliving our time together and, in the end, we have reconstructed a dialogue written over the years with them, five Cuban prisoners unjustly incarcerated in the United States.

Although sadness surrounds it, this is not a sad book. It is a testimony of faith in the fact that justice will prevail and that they will return home, where they are loved by their families, their friends and by all those who fight for their freedom. Here you will discover the human values, the altruism and the tenderness of these men who gave up their stable lives next to their families and sacrificed remaining in their country in order to defend their people from terrorist acts, organized and financed from the United States.

Gerardo Hernández, Antonio (Tony) Guerrero, Ramón Labañino, Fernando González and René González were victims in Miami of one of the most violated judicial processes in the recent history of the United States. Long before they were convicted they were classified as spies, even when the prosecution could not present any proof of such, and when several U.S. generals and military experts testified that there was no evidence of espionage in this case. But the prosecution did not have to prove its accusations, or even win the case, to have these defendants declared guilty; to secure the worst sentences for them from a jury and a judge undermined by prejudice against Cuba.

We are dealing here with men of noble ideals who were fully conscious of their acts and especially convinced of the need to do what they did. In this book the true nature of these five Cubans is reflected as well as an important part of the history of our families.

You will read, for example, the testimony of the unjust imprisonment in the United States of Olga, René's wife, in order to force him to collaborate with the prosecution, of her subsequent deportation to Cuba and of the denial of a visa for her to visit her husband and accompany her little Ivette who was barely six years old and who hasn't seen her father since 2000. You will read, too, of the love of Adriana and Gerardo, which grows in the face of his two life sentences and the prohibition on her visiting him; of the sorrow of Rosa and Fernando on learning that they can no longer have children of their own; of how difficult it is for Ramón's youngest children to maintain a relationship with their father without having him by their side; and of the willpower of Tony's mother in helping her grandchildren and her son to face this separation. You will be able to appreciate the extremes to which the rights of these prisoners have been trampled on, and how difficult this separation has been for all of us.

In the last three years those of us who have received visas have been able to travel to visit them an average of only twice a year, even though according to the regulations of their respective prisons we could have visited more often. But with ever-greater frequency the U.S. government imposes obstacles and impediments on our applications for travel. They, and we, suffer additional punishment by being deprived of regular contact.

This is a heart-wrenching book, yes, but it isn't produced with hatred, in spite of how much we have suffered. We do not ask here for anything exceptional for these five men or for our families. Only simple, elemental justice.

On behalf of all the family members:

Mirta Rodríguez, mother of Antonio Guerrero
Adriana Pérez, wife of Gerardo Hernández
Elizabeth Palmeiro, wife of Ramón Labañino
Rosa Aurora Freijanes, wife of Fernando González
Olga Salanueva, wife of René González

ALWAYS A FAMILY

René González Sehwerert

Olga Salanueva Arango

My husband, René González Sehwerert, was born in Chicago, Illinois, on August 13, 1956. He is the son of Cuban immigrants who chose to return to the island in 1961. Rene — I call him like that, without the stress in the last "e" — became a pilot and flying instructor and, in 1990, returned to the United States. When I met Rene I was working in an accounting department at the Cuban Ministry of Foreign Trade. I studied accounting and then became an industrial engineer. I had a friend whose husband was one of Rene's professors. We were introduced because they said there would be chemistry the day we met. And so it was. I was 22. We met at the beach and started to date. Within a year we were married: on April 17, 1983. A year later, Irmita was born. She and I joined him in Miami in 1996.

It was in Miami that Ivette was born in 1998, four and a half months before Rene was arrested. After the trial, he was transferred to a maximum security prison in Loretto, Pennsylvania, before being moved to McKean Federal Correctional Institution (FCI) in the same state. He was finally taken to Edgefield FCI in South Carolina, where he is incarcerated today.

Federal authorities arrested me on August 16, 2000, and I have not seen Rene since. I was held in Fort Lauderdale state prison for three months before being deported to Cuba in November of the same year. At that time I had the right of permanent residence in the United States.

The real objective of my detention was to pressure Rene into signing a confession prepared by the Southern Florida District Attorney in which he would declare himself guilty and testify against the other defendants. He refused and I was arrested a few days later. As soon as I was arrested I began to write to him. However, he never received my letters. It was clearly an effort to try to destabilize him emotionally since he did not know anything about me directly and the beginning of the trial was near.

During the period we were both locked up, Ivette remained in the care of her great-grandmother on her father's side, her dear Tata [Grandma Teté], in Sarasota, 230 miles from Miami. She was allowed to visit me only once, behind glass. Ivette, like her father, is a U.S. citizen by birth. She has not seen her father in four years — more than half of her life. I have been denied a visa to visit the United States on numerous occasions. In this case, they have violated the rules pertaining to the treatment of prisoners of the American Human Rights Convention and Article 10 of the Convention on the Rights of the Child.

I'm writing this as if I was opening a door to our lives for you. Through Rene's letters and my comments, you will witness the negative effects this unjust case has tried to inflict upon our daughters and us. You will hear of a legal system that through vile actions against a couple and their two little daughters has shown its hatred for Cuba.

When I decided to organize the letters for this book I did not know how to do it. I keep Rene's letters but he never received mine when we were both locked up. They got "lost." That's why our story here is reconstructed from his letters and my remembrances. There's no hatred. I don't know when I will see him again and visit him with our two daughters. But, I repeat, there is no hatred in me because, although it has been the cause of our separation, this has not been able to destroy us. After five years, in spite of the bars and the walls, we are still united and we will always be a family.

From René's Diary[1]
[excerpts]
Miami FDC

After individual interrogation, we were taken to the Miami Federal Detention Center (FDC) where we began our solitary confinement on the 13th floor, which at that time was unoccupied. This was a treatment especially and meticulously aimed at inflicting on us all the animosity of the District Attorney. It was designed to make our defense as difficult as possible, which in our conditions of imprisonment would play a major role... Those were the most difficult days; especially that Saturday when the solitude of my small cell wasn't enough to turn my thoughts away from my family, who had been left behind in our apartment, occupied by FBI agents after my arrest. I think that initial moment is the one that defines your attitude and how you'll deal with this new challenge that fortune has brought your way. You can throw caution to the wind, say a wrenching, painful good-bye to your life and all that you had taken for granted until then, hanging on to your principles with all your might, never giving it a second thought. Or you falter, and start looking for excuses for the betrayal you're about to commit.

Ivette was born in Jackson Memorial Hospital − the only public hospital in Miami-Dade County. We decided to keep her two surnames, González Salanueva, as I had kept mine when I went to the United States in 1996. Rene is a U.S. citizen and had arrived in Florida six years earlier. Once I had residency status, they gave me a social security number and asked how I wanted my name to appear. I kept both surnames. When Rene was arrested, they said they couldn't be sure I was his wife, since I didn't have the same

---

1. René's "preamble" for his diary, written on April 2, 2002.

last name. I had to send away to Cuba for a copy of our marriage certificate, because the original was taken from our house the day the FBI came to take Rene to prison.

The first time we saw each other in prison, the girls were our priority. We had really wanted them. When I was pregnant with Irmita, Rene and I made a wish for a little girl with dark and curly hair like mine, with big, light eyes like his, a nose like mine and so on. But when she was born, she didn't look at all like that. She looked just like Rene. We laughed a lot over that. Irmita knew the story and loved to hear it, but when Ivette was born, Irmita was jealous. She told us, "Look at her; she's just what you wished for!" Irmita was already 14 then, and had not seen her father for six years. Their reunion in the United States was very beautiful. They played together, he helped her with her homework, taught her to ride a bicycle… At first, she was jealous of her little sister who needed more attention, but as soon as she started holding and feeding the baby, her maternal instincts kicked in. Now she sees Ivette almost like a daughter.

For His Daughters
December 21, 1998
Miami FDC

For my daughters:

> Don't withdraw the smiles from your faces
> Radiant, bathed in streams of joy
> Overflowing with magical energy
> As you pass through generous spring waters
> Illuminating each day with your laughter.
> Its echo beats deafeningly within my soul
> Like a lament
> Bringing down the shameful walls
> Drowning my agony in its beauty.

To Olga
[excerpts]
August 16, 2000
Miami FDC

Love of my soul,

I suppose I have a million things to tell you, but I don't know if I'll be able to tell you even one with all these thoughts churning around in my head. It's like the first few days after my arrest almost two years ago — when you were detained, and I felt like I'd been arrested a second time. Of course, the fact that I had already gone through it helped some, since I knew that time would have a way of putting things into perspective so they don't seem so terrible as in the first few hours. I know that the first days are the worst, and that later the road opens and solutions appear. Fortunately, we have an exceptional family, both here and in Cuba, and together we'll make it through... Now that I think of it, I don't remember ever having seen one of my little women with a taciturn face in the morning.

He wrote me this letter the day after my arrest. The last time I went to visit him was August 13 — his birthday. He told me about the confession that the District Attorney had proposed to him. The plea bargain meant that he wouldn't go to trial if he entered a guilty plea and agreed to testify for the prosecution. They drew his attention to the last paragraph, which referred to his family's immigration status, letting him know that as a permanent resident of the United States, I could also be charged. Since Rene refused to sign the confession, I was arrested and jailed three days after I saw him in prison. At six in the morning when I was still asleep, three agents came to the house – one from the FBI and two from the Immigration and Naturalization Service (INS). They confiscated my green card (residency permit) and took me to the INS building in Miami. The first question was: "Where are your daughters?" Irmita was on vacation with her grandmother in Cuba, and Ivette in Sarasota with her great-grandmother, Teté. They told me that I knew about my husband's activities and that, as a result, my residency was invalid. By then, Rene had been in prison two years. I was taken to the state prison in Fort Lauderdale where the INS had a cell it used for federal cases: for inmates from the Krome Detention Center being punished for indiscipline, or for federal prisoners awaiting questioning. On the way there, they asked me if I wanted to make a telephone call, so I called Rene's uncle, and asked him to tell Grandma Teté what was happening and to tell Rene as well. She must have been very worried; the first thing I did every morning was call her. She was over 80, and looked after Ivette during the week so I could work. Rene would call me from prison for the "daily report." He was worried, knowing that Miami terrorists could harass me. At that time, there still was no time limit on calls, and moreover, they were local ones. I was also asked if I wanted to see Rene and I said yes. They spoke to me in Spanish. I guessed this would be one of the few opportunities we had left. Two hours after their offer, I was taken to the Miami FDC. They brought in Rene. They wanted to show him that they had made good on their threat and that our daughters and I were at their mercy. He looked at me and said: "Orange looks good on you!" Even in front of the guards, he hadn't lost his sense of humor. I was wearing the orange prison garb, but probably the filthiest uniform in the worse possible shape. He tried to reassure me: "Don't be afraid. They'll probably begin deportation proceedings to Cuba." We gave each other a kiss and said good-bye. That was August 16, 2000 – the last time I saw him. I didn't cry that day, although I cry quite easily. When you're among friends you cry – but not before your enemies. Dignity gives you strength and hardens you.

For Olga
[excerpts]
August 16, 2000
Miami FDC

I've just spoken to Philip [Horowitz] who told me about his visit to Fort Lauderdale prison with Julio, and about his conversation with you. Joaquín [Méndez] and [Paul] McKenna[1] are very worried and at the same time incensed with this arrogant, untimely and above all useless action against you. But I want you to know that above all else, they've told me how much they admire you for your dignity and commitment. I don't have to tell you how proud that makes me, and how it's helped me to endure the blow of your arrest. I've never doubted your values, the strength of your heart and the steadfastness of your character, but when others see it too, I feel proud, knowing that I made no mistake in making you such an important part of my life. I've always had infinite faith in you.

Irmita found out [about my arrest] when Rene's uncle called Cuba to let the family know. We decided that Irmita should stay in Cuba. My house — a little rented flat — stayed empty. Before they jailed me, I worked for a tele-marketing company selling English-language textbooks. I worked from 2:30 in the afternoon until 11 at night, and so couldn't look after Ivette and maintain the house as well. When Rene was taken away, Ivette was only four and a half months old. Fortunately, the owner of the company I worked for let me continue working there, but I couldn't miss a day. That's why I

---

1. Philip Horowitz, Joaquín Méndez and Paul McKenna are the attorneys designated by the Miami-Dade County Public Defender's office to assume the defense of René González, Fernando González and Gerardo Hernández, respectively.

decided to take Ivette to Teté in Sarasota, 230 miles from Miami. I was
allowed to visit Rene four times a month for one hour each visit. I would go
on Saturdays and then shoot off to Sarasota. From September 12, 1998,
through February 2000, all five were in the "hole" — in solitary confine-
ment. During that time children weren't allowed to visit, supposedly because
they couldn't climb up to the punishment cell. However, this rule only
applied to Rene — other prisoners were brought down to see their children.
During those 17 months of solitary confinement he only twice saw the baby
close-up. Once was in May when Ivette was 13 months old — he was
handcuffed to a chair and couldn't touch her. Then a second time without
handcuffs, since I think they realized they had gone too far the first time.
Otherwise, Rene only saw her through a glass small window they had in
the "hole." When he knew I was about to pass by, he would look through the
glass, down below. He was on the 12th floor, and so Ivette was just a little
dot in my arms.

For Olga
[excerpts]
September 1, 2000
Miami FDC

In any case, what's important is that you like what I write you, and
that every page you read brings you the message of love and support
that you deserve. Sometimes I'd like to have more time and imagination to flood you with letters, poems and messages. What I'm able
to write seems so inadequate for expressing all you mean to me in
this second half of my life, what I hope you'll be for me for the rest of
my existence. I console myself with the knowledge that every moment
we've spent together has been a time to revel in our love and to make
each other's lives happy. I know that we'll take this path again some
day, and once again — as Irmita described us when we were reunited

after six long years apart — we'll act like a pair of teenage sweethearts.

I agree when you say that there's a solution for everything, when we have so much support and love on our side and, moreover, truth and dignity. I believe that sooner rather than later, everything will be resolved and we'll finally be together with our daughters to take up our lives where we left off, with our capacity for love that half the world and much of the other half can only envy. You ask my opinion about Ivette and how we should handle things, considering the feelings of grandma and Papín [René's uncle]. I'll tell you my thoughts, as I've more or less expressed them to grandma, and I'm sure my words won't sound unfamiliar. Of course, she has also spoken to me in tears, afraid some day someone will come and take Ivette from her. I've given her my word that this will never happen, and I said that I was sure that you feel the same.

Ivette had been with her great-grandmother from four and a half months old until she was two. "Grandma" had come to have enormous affection for the baby. When she found out I was to be deported, she told me that Ivette could stay with her until I had a sure place to live in Cuba. In prison, they didn't tell me that I couldn't go back with the girl. They said the deportation proceeding was against me, and not Ivette, who as a U.S. citizen could stay in the United States. If I wanted her to come to Cuba, I would have to get a power of attorney so that someone else could bring her. It was a drama that of course involved Grandma Teté who didn't want to be separated from the child. She said that the change would be too hard for Ivette — she had become so attached to the child, and was afraid of never seeing her again. And the baby adored her, too (as she still does). But we were very afraid that they would take some kind of reprisal against Ivette, and that was something Teté understood perfectly. We finally authorized Irma, Rene's mother who lives in Cuba, to go and bring the baby back to the island.

For Olga
[excerpts]
September 1, 2000
Miami FDC

In any case, I explained to her that no matter what, the baby will continue to be part of their lives, and that we will do all in our power to make sure of that. Ivette can be brought to the United States from time to time and they can go to Cuba, too. Right now, you're the one who will have to make the sacrifice if they send you back to Cuba soon. But even so, grandma is a bit right when she says that you'll be better prepared to receive Ivette after you've had time to organize your life back in Cuba, rather than taking her with you and trying to improvise things on arrival. In fact, I think the time you'll need is about the same as from now until the end of the trial. That's why I've told Roberto [René's brother, a lawyer] that my mother should come right away, since I know you'll leave more relaxed knowing that Ivette is in the care of not only her great-grandmother but also her grandmother, who will stay in the United States until you have established yourself in Cuba and are living a more normal life. I know it's not easy at all for you to leave the baby behind, but Teté is right about this, and you'll need the time to organize your life. Once my trial is over, we can decide what to do in case your return here is prevented either indefinitely or for a long time.

If the decision is that she return at the same time as you, then have grandma spend some time in Cuba with all of you helping with the transition, with all the love and consideration that both grandma and Papín deserve. I have every confidence in the quality of our family and that love will prevail to resolve this in the best way for us all. When you write, don't forget to tell me what you think about these thoughts of mine. As to what you said about Irmita coming to say good-bye, I have no objection, but apparently it's been decided that she not come for now because, I suppose, the school year's just beginning and she has to enroll and so on. Maybe we can arrange a trip when she has a vacation or something like that, and of course I'd love to see her and give her a big hug. In any case, once the trial is over, all this will become clearer, too.

For Olga
[excerpts]
September 6, 2000
Miami FDC

A few days ago I called grandma and Ivette was dying to get on the phone. She told me lots of things: that she had hurt her leg and that Mama had cured it and put it on a pillow; that you and I were both working; that a little boy had hit her in the park because she hugged him; and all kinds of other things. It amazes me that she expresses herself as if she's already four; the emphasis she puts on some words is really funny. As she was talking, I imagined watching her and seeing her body language as she emphasized the things she was recounting. Grandma said that she talks a blue streak, and asks questions to everybody in the family. Yesterday, she said she was asking Aunt Iris why that boy had hit her in the park.

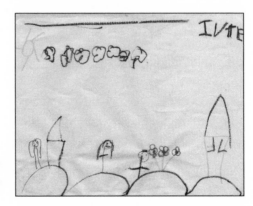

**Drawing by Ivette
for her father**

Ivette has been a little parrot ever since she was born. She spoke in both languages… At that point, of course, she wasn't aware of the difficult times her parents were going through, although when she didn't see us, she would anxiously ask when we would be back. The red tape for visits was Machiavellian: I would have to ask the FBI to grant me the favor of a visit from my daughter, which would take place in the presence of guards. Grandma and Uncle Papín would show her photos of Rene and me, so she wouldn't forget us. That's how she started to identify us, although she ended up confusing everything. Papín was adamant with the photos, and would pull out one of me every so often, saying: "This is your mother – this is Mama." Ivette ended up confused and began calling him "Mama" instead. So, he's the "Mama" that Rene refers to in his letter!

For Olga
[excerpts]
September 7, 2000
Miami FDC

Today was another visiting day and we were getting ready for inspection when they called the names of the prisoners receiving visitors again. As I've started doing lately, I looked at my little packet of candies – which I haven't tasted since you were arrested – and thought about you, and then went on with my daily routine. Although you can get used to almost everything and learn to deal with setbacks by making an effort and taking refuge in your daily routine to make you think nothing out of the ordinary is happening, I think there are inevitable moments when you remember that things have changed, and events have taken a dramatic turn. I have the impression that visiting time is one of those moments and I don't think that routine, time or habit will make me see it differently. But then, there's no harm in remembering you with a mixture of nostalgia and sadness at some specific moment of the week. Maybe without wishing it — or perhaps because I do wish it — visiting times have become another "anniversary" like the day we met, or when we were married, or when our daughters were born, something like that.

He got used to hearing his name every time those who had visitors were called. Then suddenly, it stopped. He had a little package of mint candies that he saved for my visits before I was arrested. He would hide a candy in his mouth and then pass it to me during the visit. It was our little fiesta.

For Olga
[undated]
Miami FDC

Olguita,

This poem, as you can see, was inspired by your Saturday visits:

The Week

I don't know if the sun shines brightly on Sundays
or if, on Mondays, thick clouds disperse.
I don't want to see if, on Tuesdays, sheer joy
makes the birds hop along as they sing.

On Wednesdays I don't watch the rising sun
and on Thursdays, I do not see it leave the sky.
On Fridays, don't expect to find me wondering
if the weather brings sadness or consolation.

But on Saturdays the charm of your laugh
disturbs confinement's bitterness
bursting pure into my cell, with the refreshing
breeze of your love and tenderness.

And then you go, abandoning me to the essence
of your brief presence.
A new peace, nourishing my existence,
illuminating me for another seven days.

For Olga
[excerpts]
September 12, 2000
Miami FDC

My love,

As you can see, this is an anniversary, although a sad one. It's
exactly two years since my arrest, when we were forced to separate
for the second time. Last night I was remembering that Friday, the
11th, when I was giving Ivette her milk, her big eyes fixing on mine
while she sucked the bottle. And later on, she fell asleep on my chest
with her little legs and arms open wide, just how you found us for
the lovely picture you took, which is so dear to me here. All that
changed suddenly the following morning when they knocked on
our door to arrest me. I want to confess something to you: the first
time I saw my lawyer, he told me that the trial would last between
two and three years, given the characteristics of the case. When he
told me that I was horrified! At the time, two years seemed like an
eternity, especially under the conditions of solitary confinement
imposed on us then. I could not imagine that I would spend four
months in solitary, 17 in the "hole," and that two years later, I'd be
writing you this letter still waiting for the trial to begin.

I took that picture the day before they took him away — just one day before.
I had returned from work and I saw the three of them there. I took the picture
of Rene. The baby was asleep on his chest. After I took the photo, I put the

camera on the chest of drawers. It was still there the following morning, when the FBI came, and miraculously they didn't take it. I hadn't used up the roll. When they searched the house, I looked at the camera out of the corner of my eye. Mentally, I told myself: "I won't look at it." It was the last picture of him. We never took a picture of all of us together: he took pictures of me and I took pictures of him, but never together. One day I made an appointment at a photo studio, to have a picture of the four of us together. The young man at the studio kindly recommended that we wait two or three months to take the picture since Ivette was so little that she wouldn't hardly be seen — we'd only have a photo of a little package covered with a blanket. We said to ourselves: "Yes, he's right." So we went home. A few days later Rene was arrested. We've not been able to take a family picture for five years. If the FBI had taken that camera, they would have taken a treasure.

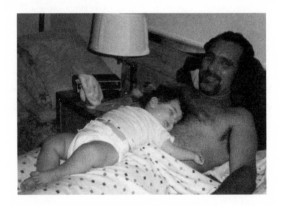

For Olga
[excerpts]
September 12, 2000
Miami FDC

I think that for us both, or rather for all of us, this has been a test, and we've come through it morally stronger. Time has flown, and it's made us better people, more mature, more united and more resistant. It seems like yesterday that we were taken to the courtroom for the first time, with that crowd of people, and Irmita gave me her confident smile. Later came your first visits in prison, when I saw your first tears. Those visits were followed by others, when we enjoyed every hour granted us, separated by glass. I'll never forget when you used to come with Ivette, so from my window I could watch her on the sidewalk 12 floors below, taking her first steps. Or the girls' first visit on May 3, 1999, when she already walked on tiptoe. Then came our transfer to the general prison population, and we could see each other in the visiting area, and I had the chance to hold Ivette in my arms, to hug and kiss you, and to take Irmita's hand. How many memories can be accumulated in two years! When I look at all this in perspective, I think that in the end, as always, our love will prevail and we'll come out of this tough test more united and loving each other even more. Some day when we look back at all this, it will be quite a story to tell, and we'll see it for what it is: a unique experience that we knew how to overcome with love, dignity and the support of so many people who opened their hearts with affection and confidence. Who, without even asking, have instinctively looked beyond the campaigns of slander and the constant lies, to understand that our nature as human beings just doesn't match that portrayal of us.

As time passed, Ivette became more anxious to see us. Once we were talking on the phone and she asked me if I was coming to see her by car or on foot. "By car," I replied and she said, "No mommy, I can see your car through the window." And it was true: my car was in front of Teté's house. Teté and Uncle Papín spoke with the prison authorities. It was a purely humanitarian matter, and the authorities promised that the visit would take place in the room where inmates met with their lawyers, so my little daughter and I wouldn't have a telephone or glass between us. But on the day of the visit, no such authorization in writing appeared, nor did the person who had given the permission. Finally, we saw each other through the glass and talked on the phone. The only thing that came to mind then was to tell Ivette that this was a hospital, and her mommy had a bad cold, and that we should talk on the phone so she wouldn't catch it, too. You can imagine how hard it was, not being able to hold her, not even touch her. Ivette asked why there were sheriffs in the hospital. Even the guards were embarrassed. She's never forgotten that visit. Every once in a while, she would remember the time she went to see me at the hospital where there were sheriffs. Fortunately, she's stopped talking about that now. That memory must be stored in her mind, but sleeping. Just like the memory of seeing Rene handcuffed to a chair. I hope that one day she'll forget it all.

For Olga
[excerpts]
September 12, 2000
Miami FDC

In the meantime, we'll continue being the keepers of laughter and optimism. We have the joy of life, the satisfaction of having gone through all this without kneeling, humiliating ourselves or giving in to blackmail, and above all, without becoming embittered.

No one will have the pleasure of saying they managed to make us resentful, for being subjected to their useless hatred. If there's something I still need to say, it's thank you, for your love, your support and for being at my side during all this time, giving me that encouragement that still accompanies me, that will always accompany me.

For Olga
[excerpts]
September 17, 2000
Miami FDC

My love,

Yesterday marked exactly one month since your arrest, the most bitter morning since my own arrest, for I called the house and got no answer and nobody knew where you were. I still remember the relief I felt when they told me that the INS had arrested you. Everything is relative, isn't it? That was also the last day I saw you, with those awful clothes they made you wear, so that there would be no doubt you'd been arrested. But even dressed like that, you were still the prettiest woman in the world for me, not to mention the one with the most dignity, which is even more important.

I spoke with Irmita and she asked me if I was able to speak with you. I explained how we communicated and I told her not to worry about you, that you were okay and that she had a mother she should feel very proud of. She told me that tomorrow, Monday, she'll be tested to see if she can begin 11th grade, and that she felt confident about it. She said that in a few days, once she passes the test, she'll resume school. I told her to visit her grandparents often, and she said she visits them a few times a week. In general she was in a good mood and optimistic, and I told her never to lose heart over these things, that all we wanted was her happiness, that she enjoy her youth and get good grades.

Then I called grandma to tell her about my conversation with Irmita and Roberto, but she had just spoken with them both, right after I had. She was a little bit tearful, because she says Ivette went crazy when she heard Irmita's voice, and that made both her and Irmita very sentimental. She says that Ivette asked Irmita when she was coming to see her, that you had told her that Irmita would come soon, etc. I can imagine how emotional it was for Irmita and grandma to see how attached Ivette still is to her older sister.

The relationship between them is very special. Before the arrest, Ivette was very attached to Irmita. Ivette used to fall asleep in Irmita's arms and when I would try to take her, she would cling to her sister, hug her tighter. It must be in their blood, that affinity. As soon as she could talk she called her sister Mita, and she still calls her that. Irmita is very special in Ivette's life; whenever she draws both of us together, she draws her sister as tall as I am. Her sister looms large in her life. According to the psychologists, that means that she makes no distinction between the love she feels for both of us, for her mother and her sister.

For Olga
[excerpts]
September 30, 2000
Miami FDC

My dearest love,
    Of course, as soon as I speak with Irmita, I'll write you to tell you
about our conversation. I'm anxious to know about her new school
and everything related with this rather abrupt change in her life —
although, in fact, this shouldn't be anything new for her.

*Irmita had finished 10th grade in Miami. She never adapted very well
there. We lived in Kendall, and her school was in another area, quite far,
where almost all the children spoke only English. She often refused to go to
school, until she began to adapt little by little, especially after she met other
Cuban and Latin American students. There, you don't visit school friends
at home, or even your neighbors. She would have to stay alone for hours in
our house until I got home from work. She used to watch television, read
and study, and started becoming a very introverted girl. That's why she
always wanted to come to Cuba during vacation. After Rene was arrested,
I started saving every penny to pay her fare. Which is why, fortunately, my
arrest coincided with Irmita's vacation on the island. She was really affected
by her father's imprisonment. She suffered anxiety and began overeating.
She began to lose her hair. It changed her character: she became more solitary
than ever and wouldn't speak with anyone. Fortunately, she never had
problems in school and had support from some of her classmates. She was
present in the courtroom for Rene's sentencing, and appeared on television
and in the papers. Some of her friends saw her and went to the courtroom to
greet her. Not only did they defy all the propaganda, but they also traveled
a long way just to see her — from Miami Beach to downtown.*

For Olga
[excerpts]
October 11, 2000
Miami FDC

Among the letters I'm enclosing, I'm including Migdalia's [Migdalia works with Olga in Cuba], on mother's recommendation, and also one from our daughter, our treasure. Although I know she wrote you too, I think it would be good for you to read the little note she sent me — so lovely, loaded with optimism and good feelings. I don't know if, as Migdalia says in her letter, we put her in a blender and mixed her so well that she ended up with our best qualities. But I do know that she has her mother's virtues, and that's enough for me. How lucky I am to have a daughter like her. Sometimes I wonder if she would have been such a good daughter if she'd had a different mother, but then I realize that I could only have children with you. How I found you, I don't really care. What really matters is that I found you in this world that seems so small for some things and nevertheless so big for others — like having been so lucky to find a woman like you.

You see how often Rene uses the term "treasures" to refer to our daughters?

For Olga
[excerpts]
October 15, 2000
Miami FDC

My love,
    I just finished talking with Irmita in Cuba, as we agreed two weeks ago. I couldn't wait to write you this letter and tell you my

impressions of our conversation. I have to tell you that our daughter is fine, doing very well. She sounded very happy and she told me that she's doing well at school, that she's adapted well to boarding school and has advanced in the subjects she didn't have a sufficient background in. She tells me that she is at the same level as some of her friends, who of course have already been studying those subjects. She told me that she had a history test, which they call a midterm or half-semester or something like that, and she got a 100. At the same time, she feels support from the whole family.

Of course, she told me she longed for your arrival and was very happy when I told her that Ivette was going to be there with you. Given her sensitivity, she immediately asked me how grandma and Papín had taken the news [of Ivette's departure], and I explained to her that they were getting used to the idea and that now nearly the whole family wanted to go to Cuba.

As soon as I arrived in Cuba, I went to pick up Irmita at school. I went directly from the airport to the school. Of course, she didn't expect me. She knew I was coming, but not when. We hugged and kissed each other like crazy, and went together to my parents' house — my father is 88 and my mother 83. They didn't know a thing. They didn't know I had been arrested and of course, they didn't expect me. Can you imagine how it was when they saw me — so thin, dressed in clothes that were way too big for me, and carrying that small bag with Rene's letters in it?

For Olga
[excerpts]
October 15, 2000
Miami FDC

The truth is that my correspondence has lately been subjected to a treatment that borders on harassment. Even Irmita's vacation diary took twice the normal time to reach me before I sent it on to you some days ago. There is definitely a plan to keep us as isolated as possible right now. But don't worry about it — just continue writing me letters as if this wasn't happening. That's what I'm doing and I prefer not to worry about what percentage of my letters you receive or not. Remember that when something is out of our hands under these circumstances, the best thing is not to get carried away worrying about it. What's important is for each of us to know that the other is doing fine, and will be fine, regardless of anybody's low-down actions.

We don't have many letters because before my arrest we spoke regularly on the phone and I visited him every week. We had more direct contact. I began receiving Rene's letters when I was arrested, although Rene didn't receive mine. Apparently they were withheld at his prison. Some were returned to me. Others were neither delivered nor returned. So I began sending my letters to his uncle, who would change the envelope and send them along with another return address. But Rene never received those either. Apparently, there was an express order that he should not receive my letters. The time I spent in prison coincided with the delay in the beginning of the trial. I was deported on November 21, 2000, and the trial began on November 27. That is to say, they wanted to keep him on edge, not knowing what was happening to me. A person about to be charged in court needs a certain degree of tranquility; certainly not the anguish of not knowing what is happening to his wife, where she is, how she is. That explains the time I was held in prison. A deportation process is usually quick. Most of the time it takes less than 24 hours. Keeping me in prison for three months was only to pressure him, to blackmail him psychologically. But he decided to deal with that situation by writing to me, not even knowing whether I was receiving his letters. I was never able to speak with him by phone. We were not granted a farewell visit.

For Olga
[excerpts]
October 16, 2000
Miami FDC

I only want to tell you that, from the bottom of my heart, I hope you're not in this situation when the third month comes around. I know that you're strong and have the dignity necessary to sustain you however long it is, but I can't wait to see you free with our two little treasures, who need their mother's warmth — and what is not warmth too. Yesterday, when I spoke with Irmita and felt that happiness in her voice, I couldn't stop thinking that among other things she should be very proud to have the mother she does. As for me, I don't have to tell you how lucky I feel that you are the mother of my girls. I will love you forever and ever.

Yours, René

I had a friend in Miami who I worked with, a good Peruvian woman who came to see me in prison. She offered to do something for us. At work we recorded conversations to avoid claims against us by customers. So we made an agreement: I called her and she recorded my message for Rene. He did the same. He called her, listened to my recording and then recorded a farewell message, telling me that he loved me, that soon we would be together, for me to take care of the girls, and that the Miami District Attorney's office wanted our family to be separated, but that they would never be able to manage that. He told me that we were together, even if we were far apart. That was the only time I heard his voice while I was in prison.

For Olga
[excerpts]
October 23, 2000
Miami FDC

Last night I spoke with my mom, and she told me that she had just spoken with you. She said you told her about the interview you had with an immigration official on the deportation process and the procedures to follow once the judge ruled that you had to leave the country. She told me you were worried that you might have to leave before our daughter's papers were in order. We talked about some ways to solve this, so don't worry about it. When the time comes, the baby will leave with you.

I had been waiting for the trial to begin, and he knew the District Attorney's office wouldn't let me be present. That's when he had the idea of keeping a diary of the trial, so I could participate anyway. He wanted to keep me away from the poisonous atmosphere of the trial itself. He was aware that the government wanted to revel in the process of my deportation − that they wanted to bring him to his knees.

For Olga
[excerpts]
October 30, 2000
Miami FDC

My love,

I can't start this letter without telling you how happy I was to see our baby yesterday − so affectionate and with those big eyes of hers that attract everybody's attention. When I got to the visiting room, my mother was with Mirta [Antonio Guerrero's mother] at the vending machines, and Ivette was talking with Margarita [Antonio's friend], at the table assigned to them at the opposite end of the room. For me it was very funny, because although her grandma was so far away, Ivette was quite calm, talking to Margarita as if she lived with her. As soon as she saw me she came running. I picked her up and kissed her. She gave me a kiss and a hug and I told her, "You are so big!" She replied, "And heavy, too!"[1] I found her answer very funny — it seems that when people pick her up they often tell her she weighs a lot.

She behaved very well and we talked a lot. She made me laugh because she speaks like the television cartoons, with the same gestures and with the same intonation. She told me that her mommy was sick, that she had a cold and that's why she couldn't hold her the day before. She told me also about the bruise on her knee and that her uncle cured her. In short, she's wonderful, and she behaved herself very well.

I'd already spoken with mom on Saturday night and she told me that the contact visit you'd anticipated so much hadn't been possible. I was worried about Ivette's reaction to the glass, but she told me that the visit went very well, and our girl accepted the explanation that you were sick and that you didn't want her to catch cold. So everything worked out fairly well after all, and I was very glad.

Ivette was two and a half years old. He carried her and kissed her. That was the last time he saw his child. She sleeps with a little doll Rene sent her from prison. It's a little brown bear knitted for her by another Cuban prisoner. It has a little, white bag embroidered with Ivette's name and filled with feathers. Ivette says it's her brother. She named it Renecito.

---

1. Ivette said "heavy" in English.

For Olga
[excerpts]
November 11, 2000
Miami FDC

I was very happy to learn from your message that you're taking the issue of Irmita very well. I agree 100 percent with you that, among other things, Irmita will be fine with you, for, as you say, she needs someone to understand and guide her without pushing — especially in her school studies. You know her well and you're right when you say that perhaps she feels pressure because of her relative disadvantage at school and that this could cause her unnecessary anxiety. I'll write her and enclose the letter with this one, so you can give it to her.

You'll have to work with Irmita to integrate her into your life, without abandoning her main task — to catch up in school. I think you'll have to talk to her a lot, and take into account her views and moods. Remember that she's a very mature young woman and whatever she thinks and feels has to be taken into account. Actually, I don't need to be telling you this, since you know her so well. You've always had such good communication with Irmita, and a relationship with her that many people would envy.

Roberto told me about your idea regarding Ivette's transfer from the family to you once your deportation takes place. I agree 100 percent with you and share your concerns. Although I can't say that all government officials I've met here are low people, it's also true that at certain levels some of them are less than honorable, and we shouldn't trust them. So I agree with what your lawyer is doing to guarantee that Ivette's transfer is carried out with the direct participation of someone from the family, and I hope this will happen.

Irmita has been able to visit Rene in prison after my deportation. She is the only person that has been able to do that. Ivette has not been able to see him, although she has spoken with him on the telephone. Rene is very cheerful and always sees the positive side of everything. Ivette likes how Rene laughs out loud, and everything she does tickles him. She's still very talkative. When the telephone rings, she dashes toward it. If it's Rene, she knows his voice right away and starts shouting "Papito!" He lets her speak, asks her questions and tries to get her to talk. Everything she says is funny to him. Sometimes there is silence, some space, and then she laughs. On the one hand, Ivette knows very well that she can't see her father because I'm not granted a visa to visit him in the United States. On the other hand, she doesn't show any desperation to go to see him in prison. She dreams of him here. She says all the time, "When my daddy comes, he'll take me to the day care center." Or, "My daddy pushes the swing hard, right, mommy?" Or, "Is it true that my daddy is tall and can reach up there?" pointing to a toy high up in the cupboard.

For Irmita
November 12, 2000
Miami FDC

My dearest daughter,

I don't know when this letter will reach you. I'm sending it to your mother for her to take when she's deported, which I hope happens as soon as possible because, with all my heart, I want her to be free and with you all. I can't wait for the moment when the three of you are together giving and receiving the love you have for each other.

You've seen how much Ivette has grown these past few months, which may seem a short time to you, but for her they're a very important part of her life. I wish I could have the chance to see how she reacts when she sees you, see how she remembers you and how much she still feels that attachment she always had for you. In any case, I know that if in any way she doesn't remember the time she spent with you, you will both catch up quickly because, as you'll see, she can give love and happiness the same way that you have been able to since you were born.

I think it's good that the three of you are together after so long — almost Ivette's entire lifetime — time that, one way or another, you've not been able to share as a family. Also, being together, you'll be able to support and encourage one another. Each of you in your own way needs to be close to the other two, to complement each other and be part of a family.

[Your mother] knows you like nobody else, and how to guide you so that you can achieve the objectives you want without going too fast, but at the same time without losing the necessary pace to catch up with the rest of your peers.

That's why I dare ask you to listen to her and follow her advice.

The important thing is that you concentrate on your goals. Do the best you can without comparing yourself to anybody, and be sure to set yourself some intermediate goals that can take you to the final ones.

I still have here all the letters I've written you and still haven't been able to send. Although we spoke with Roberto about the possibility of putting them in your mother's luggage, we decided not to because we're not sure if there will be some restriction on her transporting documents when she's deported, and we don't want the letters to get lost.

I also think it's a good idea for you to take the map you bought so you can put it up somewhere in the house and study it while you receive these letters and the others coming. As I said before, once the trial is over, we'll keep on with the geography lessons I promised you.

And also, don't forget your English. Try to read in English and don't be embarrassed to read out loud every time you get a chance. It occurs to me that now that Ivette is going there you can practice English together. It can be like a game for her, and that way you'll help her develop the language.

In short, these are some suggestions that occurred to me that might make life for the three of you a bit easier. It may sound like this old man has become a bit bossy in prison, but the only thing I can do is to share some ideas about how to take advantage of the time doing some things that apart from being useful will bring you all closer together.

Above all, the important thing is that you feel well and happy, that you take advantage of the time and don't miss a chance of either improving yourselves or relaxing. I don't want you to limit yourselves to thinking, "if daddy were here," or, "if daddy this or that." The only thing I need to know is that you are well, happy, that you feel useful and laugh about anything worth laughing about.

A kiss and all my love,

Your daddy

For Olga
[excerpts]
November 16, 2000
Miami FDC

My love,

I'm writing this letter with a strange sensation. I've never written you a letter with the vague hope you won't receive it — at least for the time being. I suppose there is a first time for everything, especially when life puts you in such unusual situations. Anyway, I trust that if you don't read it now, it won't be long until I can deliver it personally along with kisses, caresses and embraces that I haven't been able to give you for over two years, and whose urgency is accumulating. I don't have to explain to you that if I don't want this letter to reach you it's because I'm anxious for you to get out of that place and join our little treasures in Cuba once and for all.

Today, it's three months since that day when I couldn't reach you on the phone, and after so much anxiety and worry I learned, with relief, that you had been arrested. Paradoxically, who would have thought that at some point in my life I'd be happy you were arrested? That shows that everything is relative and when we find ourselves in a bad situation, the truth is that it could be worse.

One morning they came and told me: "You're leaving." I had asked the woman who shared my cell to call Teté if I was taken away, because we had agreed with the lawyers that as soon as I was deported to Cuba, my daughter would follow. And that's how it happened. Irma, Rene's mother, was ready to leave with Ivette. They took me to the Opa-Locka International Airport in Miami, after giving me the clothes I was wearing the day they arrested me. I had lost 30 pounds in three months. They put me in a little white van and transferred me to a military aircraft, together with a group of what they called the "excludables." I was handcuffed when they took me out.

They also took pictures of me before putting me on that plane back to Cuba. During those three months I was never allowed to speak with Irmita, or my mother, or Rene's family. Irma returned to Cuba with Ivette the day after my arrival there.

For Olga
[excerpts]
November 16, 2000
Miami FDC

Believe me, I've had to pluck up the courage to assimilate this idea and will forever miss the simple act of turning my head in the courtroom to find you there: erect and noble, with dignity and love bubbling over from your defiant gaze. I think one of the best virtues that have helped us in this situation is the capacity to give up so many things at once. Not having you at the trial is one more act of renunciation. As I promised before, I'll keep you informed of everything that happens each day in court.

It looks as if our desire to see each other before you leave isn't going to materialize, since you're just about to go, and I haven't heard anything about a visit. If this were the case, it's one more dream we'll have to give up. I don't need to tell you how much I wish I could see you before you go home, but after having endured two years without letting them break us, we'll be able to overcome this as well. Anyway, there's always compensation for dreams not realized. In this case, it will be when I can speak directly with you by telephone and hear your fresh voice filling me with joy and encouragement.

Be happy at all costs. Don't allow yourself a pessimistic thought or an unpleasant memory, or the trace of dejection that at some point gave you a bad moment. Think that you've overcome all these things inside and outside prison, by the strength of your character alone, your ethics and principles. Support yourself with these ethics and principles to be happy and keep your faith.

Don't deny yourself a single moment of happiness, a smile, a game with our daughters, a family meeting... If someday the shadow of my situation gets in the way of any of those moments, shoo it away! Because it won't be my figure that's projecting the shadow. As I said in my earlier letter, when you think of me, think about the time we saw each other through the glass divider on that visiting day, when I put my feet up on the counter as if taking a sunbath.

Ivette asks many questions. For example, why is my daddy in prison since he is so good? I told Rene that little by little she was going to realize what this situation was, even though I've never said anything about his cell or his jailers. When we used to go to see him in prison in Miami, I never told her it was a prison — I said it was daddy's workplace. Sometimes we would be on the bus, and she would see the detention center and say, "Mommy, look. Daddy's job." I don't want to add more pain for her. She knows her father is in a place far away and why. Rene decided to write her a letter explaining the truth, as if it were a story.

For Ivette
[excerpts]
May 29, 2002
McKean FCI, Pennsylvania

For my heart's little girl,

My beloved Ivette, I have owed you this letter for a long time now because I have so many things to say to you. Two years have gone by since we last met and we've never had the chance to talk very much, except during the four months after you were born when I presume you didn't pay much attention to me, absorbed as you were in that newborn world which doesn't leave us any memories.

Now you're already four years old, and I hear that you like your mommy to read you stories, so she'll read this letter to you until you can read it for yourself, which I hope will be soon.

I want you to know that you were born into a very happy family and a home full of joy, and your arrival, like Irmita's, was a reason to celebrate. I fell in love with your mommy the first time I saw her and soon we decided that we would create a family and stay together for the rest of our lives.

However, my duty made me come to this country where I was born, so I had to leave your mother and your sister when she was six. After another six years, they came to join me, and then you were born in the same place as your daddy: the United States of America.

This country is now the most powerful in the world. It is an empire. But it wasn't always like this. There was a time when it was much smaller, inhabited by people who had escaped from oppression. However, its government fell into the hands of ambitious people with lots of money who expanded their borders and their influence with one war after another, causing the deaths of millions of innocent people, and all to make these rulers even richer. Don't ever be deceived: the government of this country is very bad, one of the worst in history.

But notice that I always speak of the government and not of the people of the United States, who are noble and have good feelings, like all people. One should never hate any country's people, and this one has also written beautiful pages in science, culture and history. And some of them have even given their lives for Cuba.

We have ancestors in this country — good, working Americans — and we mustn't be sorry for having been born here and should respect their best traditions and their symbols. When you read José Martí, you'll see how well he was able to describe not only the faults but also the virtues of this great nation.

That is why mommy and daddy had to sacrifice their dream of being together for the rest of their lives, and that sacrifice has also affected you and your sister. I had to come to this country to stop the wicked plans of those bad Cubans and then your mommy came too, and that's why you were born here, almost four months before I was put in prison.

We were very happy waiting for your arrival, and it was like a big party for us when we knew that your mommy was pregnant. The day before you were born, your mother and Grandma Teté took me to the airport where I had to take a plane to leave for a week. Then, your mommy said to me, "I promise she won't be born until you come back." When I arrived in Texas I called from the hotel, and found out that as soon as I left the airport she had the first birth pangs.

When I returned from Texas, after a week that seemed like eternity to me, I found you looking like a big shock of dark hair with those big, beautiful blue-green eyes that look like two stars.

You made us all very happy — your mommy, your sister and me. When Irmita carried you in her arms, you always had a very peculiar way of holding on to her, very strongly, looking at her as if asking her never to put you down. I would give you your milk in the bed lying on my back with you on my stomach and with my knees up so you could rest your back. It was very comfortable for you and for me, too.

By the time I was arrested, on September 12, 1998, you were barely four and a half months old. The night before, your mommy had gone to work and I was taking care of you. When I finished giving you your milk you fell asleep on me and I decided to leave you there while I watched television. When your mommy arrived, she thought you were so cute sleeping like that — sprawled over me looking contented — so she couldn't resist taking a picture of us. That's the last one where we're together.

Then they arrested me and I could not even kiss you good-bye. When they were taking me out of the house handcuffed, all I could do was look at your mommy and give her a smile, confident and optimistic.

The government of this country unloaded on us all the hatred and evil it bears against Cuba. They put us in the worst prison conditions and they also punished our families. So, many months went by before I could see you again, and all I could do was watch you on the sidewalk across the street from the prison, where your mother used to take you and I would look down on you from the 12th floor, where my cell was. All I could see was a head of black hair, bobbing along, falling down and getting up again with your first steps.

When we were able to see each other again you were one year old, eight months had passed. We were under surveillance and when you realized that I was handcuffed to the chair you must have thought I was a dog because you started saying "bow-wow, bow-wow." Then your mommy tried to make you see what was really happening. "No, Ivette" she told you, her indignant expression sarcastic, "your daddy isn't the dog here." In spite of the conditions, we remained in good spirits during the visit.

Nine months would go by before the government, after demands made by our lawyers and facing the possibility of a scandal, let us be treated like the other prisoners and allowed our children to visit.

For some months you were able to visit me a few times. Then, the hatred of the representatives of this government again manifested itself in its meanest form. They wrote a letter suggesting that I plead guilty and at the end of it they mentioned that your mommy was in their hands, clearly threatening that they could expel her from the country if I didn't cave in to their blackmail.

As I did not, they arrested your mommy and you stayed with your Grandma Teté in Sarasota. Irmita was in Cuba and your dad and mom were in two prisons of this country. Mommy remained in jail for three months before she was deported to Cuba, and Grandma Irma had to come from Cuba to collect you to be with mommy. Your last visit was with her and I still remember you, perplexed as you stood in front of the door that would take me back to my isolation, wondering where they were taking your daddy with all those men dressed the same way. Two years have gone by since the last time I saw you.

Two years for a child your age is too much time and I can say that I hardly know you. They tell me you are very lively, talkative, stubborn, loving, active and sociable.

Your good qualities today will become your virtues tomorrow. You'll grow up in the most just society the world has ever conceived. For some years, studying will be all that this society will ask of you and you'll be able to become anything that your efforts merit.

You are growing up in a country that doesn't need to be ashamed of its past, because its struggle to be free was guided by the best traditions and the most generous and noble feelings of the human race.

I won't be able to be with you in this stage of your life, but I know that you are growing up with a family and a people that will make up for my absence. Today, you're receiving a lot of love and affection from that people, but you can't let it go to your head because all that love is proof more of their sensitivity than of any exceptional merit your father might have. Many Cubans have died heroically without even having the opportunity to write a letter like this one to their children, and you have to be very humble when a people like ours honors you as a hero.

And although I can't be there physically, I'll always support you through our family and our people. As for me, not a single day goes by that I don't think of you or that I don't try to imagine where you are or what you are thinking or if you are happy. So, my thoughts will always be with you too.

Happiness and love are the best antidotes for hatred. I keep both things for you. Lots of them. When we're together again, I'll sprinkle them all over you. And you'll once again be our little star, our fountain of joy, who that night before I was arrested slept peacefully, right next to my heart.

A thousand kisses and all my love,

Your daddy

*When somebody asks Ivette the question that always mortifies children —
"Who do you love the most?" — she replies without hesitation: "My daddy
for now, because he's the one who is all alone."*

A GOLDEN FATHER

Antonio Guerrero Rodríguez

Mirta Rodríguez Pérez

Tony was born in Jackson Memorial Hospital, Miami, on October 16, 1958. We had immigrated to the United States because my husband, also named Antonio, couldn't find work in Cuba. In November of the same year, we visited the island to spend Christmas with the family, and then came the revolution. We decided to stay. Tony was then one month and four days old, chubby and gorgeous. We called him Tonito, but I called him everything under the sun: Tonito, Tony, Guerre, Nene. That's why he signs his paintings Guerre.[1] We're a very united family, with a lot of tenderness, very happy. He grew up surrounded by love, and his own nature added to it; he was what you would call a good child. We lived with his paternal grandparents, his uncles and his cousins, all as one family. Among the three boys, he was the peacemaker. From early on, he opted for peaceful solutions. His father would chide him, "Fight back, don't take that..." and he would respond, "No, no way. I convinced him, I told him this or that." Tony always went for dialogue, which didn't mean he didn't have a strong character.

He was very attached to his father, who took him everywhere. They were always together. When Tony was 11, Antonio passed away from heart disease. That's when Tony decided to go to boarding school, and began his independent life. After finishing high school, he studied engineering — airport design and construction — at the University of Kiev (in the former Soviet Union). There, he fell in love, and when he came back he was off to Santiago de Cuba in the eastern part of the island. His wife was from there, and he went to work at the Antonio Maceo Airport in Santiago. They had a son who was also called Antonio, or Tonito. Later, they divorced.

---

1. Tony's surname Guerrero means "warrior," and "Guerre" is its shortened form.

Then he met a Panamanian woman who was related to our family by marriage. He decided to move to Panama where they were married. Their son Gabriel was born in 1992. It was a difficult period of family instability, but Tony maintained a close relationship with his sons despite the distance. Tonito and Gabriel got to know and love each other through their father. The last time I saw him "free" was in 1998 when I went to the United States to spend Mother's Day with him. It had been 40 years since I had visited the United States. Four months later they imprisoned Tony. With the drama of prison and the extreme cruelty against my son and his four companions, we have struggled for justice, but we have also tried to do right by him, taking care of his sons, bringing them closer and above all focusing on their education − something vital to their father. You can see the patience and tenderness in his letters. He writes them letters and phones them whenever he can. He writes them poems. The communication he maintains with them is extraordinary; Tonito tells his father every detail of his life, as if besides being father and son, they were also friends and confidants. It's the same with Gabriel, though because he is younger their conversations go off in a different direction.

In his letters, Tony never tells his sons about his problems in prison. Tony has digestive problems there, because he's a naturalist and vegetarian, and of course he can't follow his diet in prison. The change in diet affected him. He had a hernia, and gingivitis that went untreated, and has been subjected to cruel punishments. For example, in February 2002, when they transferred him from prison in Miami to Florence United States Penitentiary (USP) in Colorado, he was transported handcuffed in what they call "the black box," which is very uncomfortable and painful. It was a very long trip with changes of airplane, all in temperatures below freezing. He only wore a t-shirt and cardboard sandals and on arrival, they immediately put him in the "hole," with practically no clothes to cover him. He wasn't allowed to see his attorney or his family, or to write anyone, and he went without sunlight. Gabriel knew nothing of what had really happened to his father; he's been learning bit by bit. But Tonito has kept abreast from the outset. Soon, we'll go to see Antonio in prison, and we've decided to leave our tears behind in the hotel, on the plane, in Cuba. The reunion has to be a happy one, every minute we're together. After that brutal life sentence at the end of 2001, we've only seen Tony three times, and it's always been the same: when he sees me, he's full of smiles, and greets me with love and poetry. The last time we were to see each other was to be on February 14 because we were returning to Cuba the following day. Since that's the day we celebrate Valentine's Day, Tonito and I were going to put on new clothes. "Tomorrow you'll see us with clothes for the occasion," I told him. He laughed and said, "You'll have to see me in the same clothes, but I'll splash on some cologne for you." He always has something to make us laugh. But we weren't to see him again that time. A prison lockdown was declared, so we couldn't say good-bye. Even such brief moments of closeness are marked by that kind of uncertainty. He's strong and rises above things, always looking for an explanation, always holding on to a sense of justice, encouraging his sons. But there was a time when I felt very bad, when I meditated on life and asked myself why my son was being punished so badly — why I was being punished. I felt my hopes dying. I managed to recuperate, however, and now I say to myself, "No, he will return" just as his poem says — the one that has been set to music by Polo Montañez, the one everyone in Cuba knows. He's heard the song because one day I played it to him over the telephone.

I Will Return

I will return and say to life
I have come back to be your confidant.
From north to south I will deliver to the people
the part of my love hidden within me.

I will sprinkle the immeasurable happiness
of one who knows to laugh unpretentiously.
From east to west I will raise my countenance
with goodness forever promised.

For where the wind has whipped, harsh and strong,
I will go looking for the leaves on the path.
I will unite their dreams of such fortune

they cannot fly away in a whirlwind.
I will sing my songs to destiny
And with my voice, make death tremble.

For Gabriel Eduardo
[excerpts]
January 18, 1999
Miami FDC

My dearest Gabriel,

Here's a funny story about a character called "Condorito" who, as you see, is very amusing... I hope you've received some of the stories and drawings I've been sending you. They always carry a message of love for you, and tell you that you're always in my thoughts. Always remember to take care of yourself, mind your mother and study hard so your own stories and drawings will be very beautiful. A kiss and all my love from your dad,

Tony

For Antonio
[undated]
Panama

For my daddy with love from his son Gabriel, who misses you a lot
and wants to be with you soon.

For Tony
[excerpts]
January 31, 1999
Miami FDC

Tony,
  ...Your birthday is coming up March 8. If I've counted right, you'll
be 13 years old. How time flies, doesn't it? But I'm happy seeing all
you've achieved, seeing your aptitude and how mature you are. I
hope this note gets to you in time to say happy birthday! Even though
we're far apart, you know my thoughts are always with you. Have a
happy and enjoyable day with your family and friends. As always,
take care and behave yourself, and don't forget your studies and
sports. And don't forget your "golden father" who sends you a big
hug and kiss. Hellos, kisses and hugs to everyone there,
  Your dad, Tony

For Tony
[excerpts]
February 23, 1999
Miami FDC

Dear Tonito,
  I'm really glad to hear that all is going well at school, that you

liked the gardening and the work you did there. Working with soil is very healthy and useful, and you get to know how important foods are cultivated — how they grow and are harvested. And doing it with school friends makes it fun. Well done! What you told me about the gym and sports also made me very happy and proud. Sports are important for your health. Your mother and I were also pretty good at sports — or at least we tried to practice as many as we could — basketball, volleyball, and for me especially football and baseball, which were my favorites.

I don't want to end this letter without touching on something, as if we were talking face to face. When one reaches puberty (usually after around 12 years old), one feels grown-up, more independent, more responsible... Parents always say, "adolescence is a difficult age," but I think this is more of a myth than reality. The basis of understanding between two people is communication, talking to each other, getting to understand and respect each other (father to child, grandparent to grandchild, cousin to cousin and so on, with everyone). When you go somewhere, let other people know where you're going, who you'll be with, and what you'll be doing. None of this means you're any less adult, or independent or mature than others who don't bother to. On the contrary, you, your mother and grandmother will feel better, more relaxed and have more confidence in each other. Okay, I've almost finished this letter, feeling more like we've talked. We need that, don't you think? I know that we both remember [each other] lovingly, living again the times we spent together at the zoo and amusement park, times that make us today both golden father and son for each other.

[Antonio]

All his life, since he was born, all that my son Tony has given me is a lot of love, love supported by strength and encouragement. We have had to separ-

ate on many occasions, since he was an adolescent. I never got used to it and I never will; but he has taught me to have the necessary strength to carry on in spite of good-byes. He is strong and young; he has the courage of young people. I, being an old woman, always think of the time I have left to live but he has taught me not to worry about that. He tells me to think of the present and what we have lived together and it is upon that foundation of love that we remain together: Tony, his sons and me.

For Tony
[excerpts]
June 21, 1999
Miami FDC

My dearest son,

I've thought a lot about you wanting to go to a boarding school that specializes in the sciences. I think it's a good idea as long as you're sure it's what you want. You know I spent part of my high school in a science boarding school in Havana, and those were unforgettable years. Maybe telling you about my experiences will help you make your own decision. I was just your age, 14 years old, when, like you, I got it into my head to go to boarding school. Telling you this, I pretend to make you reason out some important things. Maybe you got inspired and are telling me your opinions on the matter. I repeat to you again, I rely on what you decide, and you can always count on my support and consent. I only wish things happen for your good and as you wish. Your mother will have told you that I'm in a detention center right now, awaiting trial on charges of which I'm innocent. I'm not going to recount the whole story to you because I don't think it's necessary or important. I only want to give you the assurance and peace of mind that I haven't committed any crime. I haven't done anything over which we should lose sleep. My health is good and as you can see I spend my time writing letters, poetry and stories that carry love and, I hope, add a little joy to people's lives.

[Antonio]

We have each other and we are a family in every sense of the word. On the few occasions we have seen each other after he was imprisoned or when we speak over the phone, we have a maxim that gives us strength: "A lot of health, a lot of optimism and a lot of faith." We finish our letters with those words, and also, with a lot of happiness. He says it in a poem: "That in my truth dignity cohabits / that in my love happiness always comes."

For Tony
[excerpts]
June 21, 1999
Miami FDC

Son,

These things happen sometimes, but only people guilty of crimes need fear the consequences. People like me, who are innocent, honorable and good, feel free and happy no matter where we are. I feel better and it raises my spirits to talk with you like this, openly. That's how it should always be, so that like my letters and poems say, we always should have mutual confidence and truth between us. Right now, I can't send you a present, even for your birthday. But I know you understand. And we still have other ways to show our love and pride in each other, through our letters and phone conversations, and the stories and poems we've written each other in the past few months. I trust you and, as I've said, I'm sure that knowing these things won't change your joy in life or your direction. In fact, what I most want from you right now and always is for you to be happy and proud, and to continue reaping successes in your life, with serenity and courage. Every one of your achievements I feel as my own, and every joy of yours a joy of mine, so that if you want to make me happy, be happy yourself. Does that make sense to you? Sometimes I try to imagine myself at your age, because we're alike in so many ways.

[Antonio]

There is something very important in the relationship between Tony and his sons and that is their confidence in the fact that the truth about the Cuban Five will find its way. The optimism, the will and the strength of my son as well as the way in which he tells his sons, Tonito and Gabriel, about his childhood are very important and have served to bring him closer to them. Tony was an excellent student, loved by everyone because he loved everyone... He was already "the poet" when he was studying at the Vladimir Ilyich Lenin Pre-University School. And who doesn't love a poet?

For Tony
[excerpts]
June 26, 1999
Miami FDC

Tony, my dearest son,

It made me immensely glad to get your letter and Father's Day card, and your words full of a son's love for his father moved me deeply, and made me very happy. When we spoke on the phone the other day, and you told me your grades, you have no idea how happy that made me — it was like an injection of happiness. But your openness with me has made me even prouder, to read how you've changed and matured in your attitude toward school and extracurricular activities.

Today I woke up thinking about you, and the muse (do you know what the muse is? Look it up in the dictionary, okay?) brought me a poem I'm dedicating to you. So many of my poems are inspired by you... Take care of yourself, and I will, too. Your golden father is fine in everything — health, etc. I hope and wish the same for you. With all my special love, my golden son,

Your dad, Tony

I told him that I had showed the book of poems he sent on Mother's Day to some of my neighbors. Do you know what he suggested? He told me to organize some kind of club in my neighborhood's grandparents' circle, where I could read the poems to other older fathers and mothers, like me. It was wonderful. They showed so much love, especially the grandmothers who decided to look for more poems and even to write them. We meet every year in what we call the Peña del Amor (Group of Love) and he always sends a poem for the occasion. With those virtues, with the patience that he has, with that love for his sons and for everyone, anyone can realize that my son Tony can do no harm to anybody.

For Tony
[excerpts]
August 22, 1999
Miami FDC

I would want to tell you that my uncles sent me two photos of you, Maricarla and Carli [his nephews], and I was surprised to see how tall you are. Now I understand why you tell me that you've won a lot of basketball games — you have the physique, and the skills too, I imagine. Another thing I noticed in the photo is that we look a great deal alike — so, as the saying goes: "you can't deny that you're your father's son." But you also look like your mother in some ways, so you have half and half as it should be. But this similarity goes beyond physical aspects, since your character reflects some positive traits from both — you're studious, intelligent, warm (but with a bit of that temper that your parents have, too), happy, responsible, organized, sociable etc., etc. (all the etceteras being good ones!).

If I were to give you one piece of advice that I'd always like you to remember, I'd tell you always to be a modest person, willing to help anyone who needs it, and above all, to be just. These are qualities that win friendship, but more importantly, respect. Honesty is a person's best quality. People who are dishonest will never be brave. Finally (not to bore you with my fatherly "sermons"), always trust in and communicate with your parents, with your mother and me or with another relative you trust.

[Antonio]

For Antonio
[excerpts]
[undated]
Santiago de Cuba

Dear dad,

I'm fine, and I have faith that everything will be okay. I trust you and I'm also very proud of you and your *compañeros*. I got good grades on my final exams, so I ended the school year fine, like you'd wanted and will always want. I love you very, very much,

Your son, Tonito

For Tony
[excerpts]
August 22, 1999
Miami FDC

Now that we're talking about short stories, I should tell you that Maggie [Antonio's friend] sent me a very interesting and beautiful book of stories, a compilation of what they call "literary classics" by several famous writers in the Spanish language. I'll note some of their titles, and also their authors. Here's the list (you probably have studied some of them at school):

- Miguel de Cervantes (he's the famous author of *Don Quixote*) and the short story I read was "The Power of Blood"
- Don Juan Manuel, the story is called "About What Happened to a Young Man Who Married a Very Wild, Unruly Wife." This story is terrific.
- "Lazarillo de Tormes," Chapters I and III, anonymous
- Pedro Antonio de Alarcón: "The Stub-Book"
- Ricardo Palma: "Friar Gómez's Scorpion"

- Emilia Pardo Bazán: "The Revolver"
- Leopoldo Alas: "Clarín"; "The Substitute"
- Benito Lynch: "The Sorrel Colt"
- Jorge Luis Borges: "The Shape of the Sword"
- Camilo José Cela: "Sansón García, Traveling Photographer"
- Juan Goytisolo: "The Guard"

I think reading is a very good and useful pastime and one should get used to reading books.

I'm hoping to teach you a love for reading, but you'll have the final say. I'll tell you, once you get in the habit, you'll find that books can be very entertaining and teach you a lot.

[Antonio]

For His Sons
November 8, 1999
Miami FDC

When I See You

> *We go to restore much that we lost*
> *We go to make the most of the little we have left*
> — *Mario Benedetti*

How many elapsed days and nights
have not been desirable or precise enough
to lock them up with my dreams;
yet without you, I have counted them all.

I know the future will come and other days will come
and this second will be left behind,
other days to trace a plan of happiness,
to define what we will do with the world.

I know we will commence restoring time,
stitching the wounds and pathways,
making the most of what we have left together
and it will be when I see you and you say to me:
everything is as when you departed,
everything, as before, awaited your coming.

For Tony
[excerpts]
November 14, 1999
Miami FDC

Tony, I'm told that you're going to school in the countryside next
Tuesday. I hope you're excited and that you enjoy the experience.

Don't forget to write me and tell me how it went: your experiences, what you did, what you liked and what you didn't like. I'm sure that you'll take care of your asthma, and won't have any problems. So, congratulations on your decision, and I'm glad to see you joining in activities that contribute to your development and maturity. You tell me that computer science is a new subject this year. Nowadays information technology is vital for all of the sciences, and also for humanities, and for work in offices, warehouses, accounting, economics, statistics, etc. So everything you can learn about it will be helpful to you in the future... Take good care of yourself. Always remember to behave yourself, help out at home in whatever you can, and think things through before you do or say anything, so that they turn out better for you. Always loving you infinitely,

Your dad, Tony

For Tony
[excerpts]
September 26, 2000
Miami FDC

My dear son, Tony,

I imagine that you're doing fine in your new school. Changes always give you new motivations, and the jump from junior to senior high school is a big one in everybody's life: a new school, new teachers, new classmates, in short a whole different world from junior high. I know you'll still get good grades, and join in all the school activities — that you already have your own sense of responsibility. I don't know if you and your classmates are already doing agricultural work in the countryside. I know that this is a hard test for you, given your asthma, but it's a very useful experience and you'll learn things that will be helpful to you, especially that nothing drops from heaven — rather, people have to work to provide the food that is essential for life. Work is good for your upbringing, and being lazy, one of those people that enjoys the easy life, is no good at all. From early on, it's important to enjoy work and value its importance for society. I think that work is the key to real happiness, and it's also the contribution you can make for the other people who share our planet. I'm telling you all this — things I'm sure you already know — since I think young people should be aware of the world around them, learn what is fair, humane, really necessary and useful and keep from developing a consumer mentality, or letting greed and individualism overtake them.

[Antonio]

For Tony
[excerpts]
April 1, 2001
Miami FDC

My dear son,

I hope that by the time you receive this letter you've finally received my previous letter, which has taken a long time to get to you. I got your letter, the one you sent me on February 19, and as always it made me very happy. You can't imagine how much each word of love, trust and encouragement from you means and is worth to me; they cheer up me, make me happy and have a special place in my mind and in my heart. In each letter you send me I try to imagine and discover who you are, how you're doing, your needs, and your likes and dislikes. I try to get a better idea of the environment surrounding you, how you live, how you're maturing, what's important to you, what you're doing and what responsibilities you have. So, reading your letters, I'm always looking for the answers to all those questions — the list is a long one! I must confess I am a very happy father because your letters are open and eloquent, sincere and spontaneous, and above all, they are well written, with a lot of love. So I can be closer to you with them. José Martí said: "Words have to be brilliant like gold, light like a wing, solid like marble," and I find your words like this when you write me and when we talk.

[Antonio]

For Antonio
[excerpts]
[undated]
Santiago de Cuba

All the family knows that these are the most tense and bitter moments of this process, but we also know we have to face it fearlessly and firmly, thinking always that one day, justice will prevail — like the many other times when it comes to things having to do with there and here, as you know. I say all this, dad, because everyone in the family gives me advice, and I've always had you and my grandpa in my mind — now I only have you left. But in spite of the distance, you're with me. I know I don't know how to do everything as well as you, but I try to be like you. You're the person I most want to be like, and I'm always thinking of you.

Here's a big kiss and all my support, dad. From your son, who loves you,

Tonito

For Tony
[excerpts]
April 1, 2001
Miami FDC

There's no reason to be sad — try to feel like I do, proud and happy that no matter what our situation is, we know how to find joy in life, that we love each other and above all, continue to be constructive. It's been a long process — the trial itself has already gone on for 72 days, a long time for any trial. But let me tell you that all this time, there's not a day that I've felt pessimistic, sad or depressed. I haven't felt defeated, not even one day have I felt like a guilty person, or lonely, because I know that hearts like yours have been with me, and always will be.

Just the opposite. Every day I am happier because every day is a reason to be happier and to give more of myself. Every day I know I am closer to you, not only because all of this will end some day, but also as time goes by we understand each other better, we look more alike regarding our way of thinking, seeing life, understanding the world.

[Antonio]

For his sons
June 30, 2001
Florence, Colorado

You Are

To my sons

You are my hand
if I cannot greet faraway friends.
You are my voice
if I cannot denounce in the round tables of ideas.
You are my smile
if I cannot console in the purest hour.
You are my dream
if the moment arrives that I cannot dream.

For Antonio
August 28, 2001
Panama

Dear dad,

Dad, I love you very much, and I've been thinking about you. I want to ask you how you are. I'm very well. I'm in a scout troop, and they gave me a uniform.

Dad, I hope that you're well. I'd like to see you. I love you, dad. Your son, Gabriel Eduardo Guerrero Pérez

Dad, I forgot to tell you about my school. I'm doing very well. There are some subjects that are hard: science, music, mathematics and domestic science. Good-bye dad. Come back soon.

Dad, I love you very much.

For Tony
[excerpts]
[undated]
Miami FDC

I want to begin by commenting on your letter — father to son, or good friend to good friend, or what's better, best friend to best friend, which is what we are. Just like you, I often think of all these years that we haven't been "physically" together. And I say "physically" because it's true that we haven't personally shared all this time, but "mentally" we've always been together. Time has passed really fast, so much so that sometimes when I look back, as the song says, "it seems like yesterday" that we played together at the amusement park and the zoo. But the truth is that instead of carrying you or having you ride on my shoulders, it will soon be you who's able to carry me with your young, strong muscles. A giant, indestructible love was sewn between us during those years. Indestructible, that love never died, and will never die.

[Antonio]

For Antonio
September, 2001
Santiago de Cuba

Dear dad,

First of all, I want you to know that I'm writing you this letter, knowing that three days ago, it was three years since they put you in prison in Miami. I know that all this time, you've shown that you're a man of honor, with high moral values. I want to talk to you about the terrible thing that just happened in the United States, that has been such a terrible tragedy for so many people. Our government's willing to give whatever help is needed, since so many innocent people lost their lives and families. On the home front, I've been a little bit lazy, though I try to help mom whenever I can. She wrote you a letter. My Grandma Irma sends you a kiss — she loves you very much and is holding up. We all have our fingers crossed so that everything turns out how we all want, how you want. The neighbors and especially the people who worked at the airport with you all send their best, and they hope to see you here as soon as possible.

I miss you so much and sometimes, I'm a little sad for what you may undergo,

Your son Antonio Guerrero, Jr.

For Antonio
October 29, 2001
Santiago de Cuba

Dear dad,

I write this letter to you from the Segundo Frente municipality, where I'm working with my classmates. I'm feeling good, and working to collect the three cans of coffee beans that we aim to collect every day. On Saturday afternoons, we usually play baseball in the campground, and the girls watch us play. Every time I go to bat, I say to myself, "Here comes Antonio Guerrero to the plate!" and I try to act like you or my Grandpa Antonio, even though nobody knows, just me. So every time it's my turn, I think of both of you, and I hit that ball as far as I can. I have to tell you that I haven't had a girlfriend here, but I'm feeling good and get along with all the girls fine. One or two have come up to me and told me that one of their friends has her "eye on me," but I've told them to wait a little bit to give me a chance to make up my mind, since that's happened more than once. And later today, as a matter of fact, I'm set to meet up with a really pretty girl. I read your letters, and they moved me a lot. Please tell your *compañeros* that I liked the card they sent me. I love you and miss you,

Tony

For Tony
December 28, 2001
Miami FDC

Tony, my son,

I'm very proud to see how worthy and brave you've been, hearing of the unjust sentences handed down to your five fathers. You were with me when I stood to read my statement yesterday. You're always in my heart and mind, like your brother Gabriel. Study hard and remember that this is your main responsibility, and don't forget your manners. Always help and love your mother. I won't say more, since I know you're doing everything to be a young Cuban man — revolutionary — worthy of these times. Give all the family and friends my best. Tell them I wish all of them — as I wish you — a very happy new year, and congratulations on the 43rd anniversary of the revolution.

A special hug from your five fathers,

Your dad, Tony, your Uncle Fernando, your Super-Uncle Gerardo, your Father-Uncle Ramón and René (the Best Uncle).

For Tony
February 17, 2002
Miami FDC

Tony, my dear son,

We've been forced into a long silence, and haven't been able to talk since the end of January. I haven't been able to call you again, but we're both already immune to those problems, and we know how to resist and overcome them, since we know that neither distance nor time can erase the love that binds us — love you've described as a "golden love" between a father and a son who always try to be as valuable to each other as that precious metal. This letter will not be very long but my infinite love goes with it. All my best and a big hug to your Grandma Irma, your mother and all the family, neighbors and friends. I send a big hug for everyone. And, of course, I have to give you some advice! Take care of yourself, study as hard as you can, help your mom, be happy, modest, discreet and simply be yourself. Don't forget that you can count on your golden father for anything. The best hug and kiss from your dad,

Tony

For Tony
[excerpts]
April 4, 2002
Florence, Colorado

José Martí said: "Every day in a person's life is an indelible page of history." So live every day giving the best of yourself, and you'll see that today will be happy, and full of hope.

[Antonio]

For Gabriel Eduardo
May 2002
Florence, Colorado

My dearest son, Gabriel Eduardo,

I don't know when your mother will give you this letter — she'll know to pick the best time. There's a reason why I haven't been able to see you for so many years. I hope that you'll forgive me for not telling you sooner, but you were too little to explain things to. Since 1998, I've been imprisoned in the United States as a result of an injustice that one day you'll come to fully understand. Your father has

never committed a crime, never hurt anyone or anything. I've always been a man who acted the right way — just, human and modest. But above all, loyal to my principles and convictions. I have been tried and sentenced, when all I did was to struggle against terrorism to keep Cuba and its people away from harm, and keep others and other countries away from harm as well. My hope is for you to grow up to be a good person, useful to society, loyal to a true and worthy cause. Thus, you'll need to study hard, since knowledge will help you to understand and shape the world around you. The most important thing is that you be a generous person, since individualism and egotism aren't worth a thing. "The person who gives of himself grows." As Che said to his children: "Above all, always be able to feel deeply any injustice committed against anyone anywhere in the world." Be honest, just, brave, and you'll always be respected. Love your country, Panama, and your people; just as one day, I'd also like you to love Cuba and her hospitable and heroic people. I hope that soon, you'll get to know your brother, Tony. He loves you with all his heart, just like your little brother Alex does. You'll see. We'll see each other soon, be sure of that. And we'll never stop loving each other. The biggest kiss and hug in the world from,

Your dad

For Tony
[July 25, 2002]
Florence, Colorado

From Your Childhood

Playing in the park,
Whirling wooden horses.

I took you, as a child
endlessly round and round
on an elegant steed
one summer afternoon.

Cutting through the air
your mischievous little hand.
We returned after dark
beneath a shower of stars.

Joys of your childhood
preserved along the way,
an amusement park,
a horse on the carousel!

For Antonio
August 23, 2002
Santiago de Cuba

Dear dad,

I'm writing again to tell you about my summer vacation, how I'm
doing with Diana, how things are going here, and the preparations
I'm making for school in the countryside; all of this to spend a nice
time together learning how things are going on. This has been the
best vacation since you were last in Cuba, and I don't say that just
because Diana was here with me, but because the time was so peaceful that it brought back memories of the first time you went to my
school, for sixth grade graduation, and later when we went to Havana
and had such a great holiday together. Here in Havana, I heard
some of your poems put to music by some of our best performers,
and they were so good that I really got emotional. I can't wait for you
to hear them, too, and you can even dance a little with the phone

right next to your ear. Wouldn't that be original? Your son, who loves you, follows your footsteps and misses you,

Antonio Guerrero (El Junior)

P.S. El Junior, that's what some friends call me now. What do you think?

For Tony
[excerpts]
August 24, 2002
Florence, Colorado

Tony, my dear son,

Summer vacation is almost over, isn't it? As I said before, I know they've been unforgettable, maybe some of the most important days of your life. I hope you've not only enjoyed yourself, but that you've also learned a few things that will be useful later on.

I have done nothing else but fulfill my duty in the most natural and correct way. Millions of Cuban men and women would have done the same in my place because we have a great and old tradition of true, altruistic and intelligent leaders, those that, like Martí said, did not stand to look where life was easier but where their duty lay.

Please, don't see me as a hero and don't talk about me like someone who is better than anyone else. Picture me as someone who is just doing what he should, and as a father who tries to guide his son and be an example for him. Never try to lean on my or someone else's virtues to become somebody. Be yourself. It's very important to be yourself — to be sincere and modest, to know how to listen to people, and to always be ready with a helping hand. We're like our poems. You are: the hand, the voice, the smile, the understanding, the poet and the dream that represents us wherever we may be.

[Antonio]

Antonio wrote to me: "Trust me like I trust you and be happy and proud because your son will not disappoint you." That's how he is, an affectionate son, a loving father, a man of peace. Justice will find its way some day and I am confident that I will see him here again, for him, for me, for Tonito and Gabriel, for those who need him and for all those who fight for his return. These years of cruel imprisonment have been difficult but they have also showed me his human value and it has taught me that, no matter the distance and the conditions, a father can be very close to his sons. Gabriel has not been able to visit him in prison although Tonito has. It was a memorable moment the first time they met in prison. The first time we were together in Florence (Colorado) — Tony, Tonito and I — five years had gone by since Tonito had seen his father for the last time. It was really something. Tonito cried and hugged Tony who could not stop saying: "Look at my son, this is my son."

For Tony
[excerpts]
[undated]
Florence, Colorado

My love for you has grown, grows and will continue to grow. Ah! It's true that when you look around you don't see that great person, as you say, me, your golden father. But my absence isn't real, since you know that I'm always thinking about you, and I'll never abandon you, nor will I ever give up supporting you and giving you my advice. Instead of seeing me as absent, find me in everything you do, in your studies, your basketball games, the meetings with your friends and family, in your conversations with your mother, with your grandparents, your cousins and uncles. Let's make a pact, a pact that is fair, intelligent and also useful. One that will make us both happy. Starting right now, I'll be "your golden, fresh-air father" and you'll be "my golden, fresh-air son." That way, we add the "fresh air," so that we share the air we breathe, and it circulates in both our lungs. Do you agree? I'm sure you will. I imagine you've already seen the latest pictures of your brother, Gabriel Eduardo. As you can see, he's much bigger, and I'm sure you've found he looks like you. Besides being intelligent, kind and affectionate like you, he's also good-looking and likable like you. I phone him once a month, like you, and write him letters and postcards. He's fine and doing great in school.

[Antonio]

For Antonio
[excerpts]
[undated]
Santiago de Cuba

Even though I'm not a poet like you, I'll write something to see if I can be like you, because if there is somebody in this world whose example is worth following, it's you, my golden father.

[Tony]

For Tony
[excerpts]
November 1, 2002
Florence, Colorado

Why does terrorism exist? Mainly because people don't love each other, because they don't respect other people. Only love and respect can put an end to the hatred and terrorism that has caused so much suffering on this earth.

Son, I've given you a "sermon" on this topic — which I am related to — in part because for many years, the time we've been separated, I've devoted my life to trying to prevent such terrorist acts and the death and suffering they bring with them, to our people and other peoples.

There's something else I wanted to talk with you about; something very important and interesting for you. It has to do with what you are planning to study once you finish high school. I could give you my ideas but I think that your own inclination is what's most important. When I was about your age and I was going through the same dilemma, one that all students have, I decided for myself what I was going to study. I had the support of my mother, who has always encouraged me. I remember that the year I finished, only two spots were assigned for the whole school, even for the country; it was a special opportunity and a responsibility at the same time. Thanks to my academic record, I was one of the two chosen. I felt very happy the day I saw my name on the list saying that I'd been selected.

In any case, you're the one best able to decide what you want to study.

And thinking about this will help you to understand another important thing — that whatever you decide, the main thing you should concentrate on is being a useful person wherever you are. Because it's not only about getting a degree. It's about being able to develop what you study, and that's only possible when you're clear that you need to be useful wherever you are, and do your best for the cause you believe in.

[Antonio]

For Antonio
February 8, 2003
Panama

Dear dad,

I wanted to send you this letter and ask you how you are doing. I'm fine, having a wonderful time with my aunt. I went to the beach in Colón last Sunday and ate sausage and fried plantain. On Monday I went to the river and I had a lot of fun. Dad, I hope you liked my letter. I wish you good health and I hope you do fine too.

From your son,
Gabriel

For Gabriel Eduardo
May 21, 2003
Florence, Colorado

My dear son Gabriel,

We have not been able to talk too much this month over the phone since I was in an area where there were no phones and I had to go very far away and I did not have time because of the work and other activities here, but I always think that you are doing fine because I know that your mother and Javier take good care of you. You should always think that I am okay too.

Your family in Cuba is already preparing everything for the holidays. They are very happy that you will be there with them and you can go to the beach, parks, restaurants and other places. I am sure that you are going to like being there a lot and you are going to be very happy. I think that someday soon we will have our own holidays together and we are going to have a lot of fun. Have no doubt about that.

Your daddy always thinks of you and loves you so very much.

Whenever you have time and you feel inspired write something to me — that makes me very happy. I want to know about your school, your schoolwork and your friends.

Big kiss,

Your daddy

For Tony
[excerpts]
[undated]
Florence, Colorado

I want to tell you what I think about the need you said you feel sometimes (or daily) to have me near. I understand you, and think like you do that it would be wonderful for both of us, but life has put physical distance between us, and challenged us to be united despite that. To be happy, despite our separation — something we've been managing better every day, no matter how adverse the conditions.

I'm going to tell you a little bit about me. Maybe these are things you already know, but maybe it will help you to see how sometimes in life, we have to learn to keep going by ourselves — and when we're surrounded by love and the support of a good family, all the better. I was only 12 when my father, your grandfather Tony, died. You can't imagine how close we were. I used to go with him to voluntary work and to baseball games at the stadium. He tried hard to teach me how to play baseball — I think his dream was for me to become a baseball player. But, above all, he taught me to love the revolution and be an upright man.

Don't be afraid of setbacks or indecision. More than anything, they teach us and make us more mature — a process I think lasts a whole lifetime. We always learn something new, because we're always living new experiences — otherwise, what would life be? Everything is a lesson to grow, so it's good to know good and bad things.

Once we start to see life as giving to others, being at the service of someone or something, a worthy cause, then suddenly we realize that we barely have time enough to do everything we want, that we think is worthwhile and that makes us happy. Take care of everything around us: a flower that might be insignificant to others, putting a smile on somebody's face, offering a hand to a friend in need, reading a book that teaches us something, helping our loved ones with the housework. These are little things that can make you glad at heart, and also, as I've said before, keep us busy and useful. Remember that material things are not the fundamental things.

I understand how hard it is for you to deal with the difficulties in our communications, but if we manage to make it constructive and powerful, we'll feel fulfilled and satisfied with what we have.

When someone shouts at you or asks you questions — for the fact of being my son — answer them simply as a revolutionary young man, proudly and modestly; make them realize you are nothing more than a revolutionary young man, part of our heroic people, one who does his best, not for his father, but for the just and worthy cause he defends. Were my comments useful for you? I hope so.

With all my fatherly love,

Your dad, Tony

A HUMAN BEING LIKE ANYONE ELSE

Fernando González Llort

Rosa Aurora Freijanes

The first time I could visit Fernando in prison in the United States was at the end of April 2002. We had not seen each other for three years and 10 months and we'd had no communication at all for 27 months. He had already been sent to Oxford, Wisconsin. Since he gets a certain number of points equivalent to a limited number of visiting hours, I traveled at the end of one month and returned at the beginning of the next, to take advantage of two month's points. Fernando was reclassified when he was being transferred from one prison to another. Initially, he had been sent to a prison with fewer restrictions, but he was punished again. They sent him to a maximum security prison with incarceration conditions far more difficult than the institution the Cuban Five had originally been assigned. When I saw Fernando, I was shocked. He was much thinner than the last time we said good-bye in Havana. But he was firm, serene and optimistic, with a strength I didn't know he had. The conditions are very hostile, but he faces them with the absolute certainty that he is defending a just cause. Fernando is of medium height, with a round face and always a little overweight. He had lost at least 30 pounds. Imagine the atmosphere: the prison is in Oxford, a place close to the Canadian border with nearly nine months of winter. It's located at the end of an interminable road, where you only see rows and rows of pine trees. You sit in a cold, empty room and wait until they bring you the prisoner. Each one files in through a door with a small window that doesn't let you see a thing, but still you can't stop looking. Two or three inmates had come out and I didn't know what I would do when I saw Fernando, if I would cry or start to tremble. Just then, the door opened and I saw him. A guard stood at his side. He opened his arms as wide as he could, gave me a smile from ear to ear, and didn't give me any time to react. We embraced and it felt so natural, so beautiful, so relaxed, as if we'd only parted a

couple of weeks ago or he was coming home from a trip to the provinces. My
anguish faded away, and I still don't know if I cried or not. I don't think I
had the time. The only thing I remember was his smile and his cheerfulness.
He never complained. You won't find a single complaint in all his letters.
He was keen to hear every last detail about my life, and spoke to me softly
without dramatizing things. In that first visit, we didn't speak of the children
we wanted to have.

For Rosa
[excerpts]
[undated]
Miami FDC

My *flaca*,[1]
   ...I want to get this letter off to you if I can, even though I haven't
written the rest of the family yet. The reasons are obvious — I want
the things I've mentioned in this long letter to reach you as soon as
possible. Because I've had so much work with the sentencing process,
I haven't had time to write everyone else. Would you explain this to
them, and share with them the parts of this letter that refer to things
that I know they, too, are worried about and want to understand.
   Don't think I've forgotten that December 25 is your birthday. I
know that you don't want the years to go by, but it's inevitable. Once
more we have to spend the day physically separated, but that won't
stop me wishing you all the happiness you deserve and reassuring
you again that we'll have the time to recover what our physical separation hasn't allowed us to enjoy together. And such a separation
won't keep me from loving you more every day, admiring you for
your strength, your resistance, company and understanding.

---

1. "Skinny girl," a term of endearment Fernando often uses.

They read every letter. They listen to every phone conversation. That's why we hold back. So our private life isn't shared there. I say to myself: there are so many things I still have to say, but how am I going to tell this or that to him…? Sometimes we get into fierce debates — it's hard for me to openly express my feelings. I'm not comfortable with that. But when we're face to face, I become overwhelmed about something that is not new, something logical for a couple that loves each other: having children. We wanted to have children, but we wanted to raise them together. Anyone who knows Fernando understands his desire to manage things in the family, to participate in experiences that are vital for our lives together. We'd spoken about this in the prison. Nonetheless, we decided to have children against all odds. Even with him locked up so far from home.

For Rosa
[excerpts]
[undated]
Miami FDC

My love,

Telling me about situations you face doesn't mean you're complaining or asking for help. You're simply seeking an opinion from the person who shares this life with you, the one who will support you as best as he can in these circumstances, who will be happy when he sees you making headway against the difficulties, or who will understand when a solution doesn't appear right away.

For Rosa
[excerpts]
[undated]
Miami FDC

My love,

Neither the visitors' list nor the marriage issue has been resolved. In terms of including you on the visitors' list, the people here have it all wrong. The unit manager who was in charge of that has been transferred to another job elsewhere, and no one has been officially named to replace him. I'm going to raise the issue again when I have my six-month meeting with the unit team, which should be soon. Then there are also the efforts being made by the consul, who approached the prison authorities offering to give them whatever information they needed. If they don't respond to him, then we'll have to follow the administrative appeal procedure. But I'm hoping it will be resolved.

As to the wedding, I'm beginning to think that the most practical thing would be for us to marry by power of attorney. After all, we don't need much, and we're prepared for anything. The important thing is to legalize and formalize our marriage. The other idea — that the consul marry us — was lovely, what I would have wanted, but they're putting a lot of obstacles in the way.

Fernando and I lived together from June 1990, but we weren't legally married. We had to go through endless red tape to marry in prison. This pure formality took months. Without telling me, Fernando began making the inquiries through the Cuban consul. He wanted to surprise me. When I found out, a wave of feelings swept over me — sad and happy at the same time. Happiness at a decision that above and beyond its formality, expressed commitment, faith and love. Yet, it was also the wishes of a man condemned to 19 years in prison. He left it up to me to accept his proposal or not, knowing what we were up against. Of course, my answer was yes. But, to give you an idea of how bitter that time was, when Fernando told the prison officer in charge of his case that he wanted to get married, the man gave him a strange look that said, "There's a woman out there who wants to marry you? A man condemned to 19 years in prison?" Nevertheless, Fernando was so excited. He wanted the consul to marry us during my visit – with a small, intimate ceremony, a party for three. It wasn't to be. Fernando had to sign a notarized power of attorney in prison and send it to the U.S. State Department so that they could then process it and send it to the Cuban Interests Section in Washington. Then, in Cuba, the family attorney legally represented Fernando, and a notary performed the wedding. It was a cold formality, far from what he had wanted. Nonetheless, I felt him there at my side.

Don't forget that there are tremendous difficulties to overcome just to visit him, which means not only granting me the visa – sometimes delayed for months and months, like now when I've been waiting a long time just for an answer. Not only do I have to live in a state of anxiety and uncertainty, waking up every day wondering if there will be news, but we also have to get permission from both the Federal Bureau of Prisons and the authorities at the prison where Fernando is incarcerated. They haven't even registered his mother on the official list of visitors he's allowed. His own mother, it's absurd, a totally unjustified cruelty. So, that's when he started speaking to me in a different tone, feeling it would be impossible that we would be allowed to have a child under such conditions.

For Fernando
[excerpts]
January 29, 2001
Havana

Fernan,

...you're here with me, even in this new house of ours you haven't been to yet. But even so, I've seen you making coffee (because mine doesn't taste very good), or bringing me a glass of water (like I always ask you to do), or watching a television show together and commenting on it later on. Whenever we talk, you ask me to take care of myself — don't worry, I do that, and more, for you...

For Fernando
[excerpts]
May 1, 2001
Havana

Fernan, who says I've lacked your support? All this time, I've felt you encouraging me to do whatever I decided, and when I've found myself in a hard situation, you're the one who's helped me face it and go on, helped me with your example. Or don't you remember when we talked about my job, for instance, and you were the one who said I could do something else that interested me more; it's you who encourages me and helps me, my love. When I go forward, I don't think only of myself, but of us both, because when I achieve something I know that it makes you happy. Because I know how much you love me, and that I love you with that same strength, my darling. You are my truth and my love — pure, worthy and loyal — and nothing and nobody can do anything against that. The fact that we are far apart doesn't mean we're separated. I feel one with you — you can count on me, my love. We're holding hands, you and I, and I'm not letting go for anything in this world. So keep giving me your support, like you've done til now, and you won't find a happier woman in the whole world.

For Rosa
[excerpts]
June 4, 2001
Miami FDC

Sweetheart,

All the letters go out tomorrow, and I realize that they'll get to you around February 14, or at least I hope so. I don't want to let the opportunity go by without telling you how much I admire you for your infinite understanding, your patience in dealing with me, and for the unconditional support you've always given me. No separation will ever mean that I'll stop loving or admiring you. I know that you must have moments of uncertainty and sometimes sadness, but don't let them get you down. Stay optimistic. Life continues on its way, time passes, and we'll come through this test stronger than ever. Nothing is stronger than our love. This Valentine's Day, I send you all my love, admiration and affection.

A kiss from your eternal love,
Fernando

For Rosa
December 25, 2001
Oxford, Wisconsin

> Of all the moments of my day,
> those I share with you
> are the most important to me,
> it doesn't matter what we do...
> Of all the happy memories
> I keep in my heart,
> the ones I cherish the most
> are those in which you are present...
> And of all the special dreams
> I may have had in my life,
> my favorite one came true
> when you became my wife.
>
> Happy Birthday!

I inquired about in vitro fertilization so that we could have a child. We wanted a child who would be his and mine. We were up against the clock — I couldn't wait all the years he has left in prison, but also, my own biological clock was ticking, and I potentially had only months. I'd done all the physical tests, and my body was in perfect shape to undergo the procedure. He knew it would be difficult, since they bureaucratize everything in prison, and the conditions and formalities are always worse for him than for any other prisoner. He asked me not to get my hopes up with the insemination, because if marrying had been so hard and it was only a question of paperwork, he was almost certain this wouldn't be possible.

For Rosa
[excerpts]
[undated]
Oxford, Wisconsin

My love,

...I'm not going to raise the issue of your health and the things you should see a doctor for. I already mentioned that on the phone, and I'm waiting for the letter where you explain the whole thing to me. But I do want to tell you — like we already said — that whatever the results might be from the tests, whatever the real possibility is for us to make our plans come true, I'll always love you as I've loved no one else in my life. Sometimes things don't always turn out as we'd like, and so I think it's up to us to accept reality and move on, with maturity and a lot of love. Life gives us many possibilities — we've talked about that — and what we need to do is to take advantage of this and be happy. If it's not one way, it'll be another, but I know we'll be happy in whatever circumstances. And by this I don't mean to say that we should give up any hope of making our dream come true. We have to fight for that dream knowing how difficult it is to realize. And if it can't be, we'll have the satisfaction that we did everything possible to achieve it, and this in itself will make us love each other even more.

When I realized that my biological clock was ticking relentlessly, I knew our children would never come. Telling it to Fernando was very hard. But I told him straight out, my heart broken. Normally, people would say: Okay, life has its ups and downs, he's young, and he can still have children. They see him, but not me. The last time I went to visit Fernando in Oxford − I've only been able to go three times in the last two years − I told him: "If, when you return, you still want children, I would understand if you wanted to separate and remarry." I couldn't be selfish. But he got mad. He said a lot of angry things − what kind of a man did I think he was, how could such a possibility even have crossed my mind. If I wasn't to have children, then he wouldn't have any either. Thus we closed that painful chapter. And we have each other, forever.

For Fernando
[excerpts]
June 30, 2002
Havana

Fernan my love,
    ...I don't know how this letter will turn out because there are so many things on my mind, I don't know how to organize them... I'm fine, in health and in spirit, a little more nervous than usual, but I know you understand that, and you know I can manage it, even though I've had some powerful feelings these past few days... But don't worry, I know one day, we'll sit by the sea and talk about these times, recount our memories, tell each other stories when you come home.
    ...Don't keep things back − tell me everything about you, and

don't leave out the details, however painful... I know that you want to keep me from suffering, but don't worry, even though I've had times of anguish and pain because of our separation, I've thought later how necessary your presence is there for the good of all, and I repeat once again that the pride I feel makes me give thanks to life for allowing me to share my destiny with the special man that you are.

For Rosa
[excerpts]
[undated]
Oxford, Wisconsin

Rosa, yours is that kind of anonymous heroism, that silent comprehension, unconditional support for the cause worthy of admiration, and which makes me proud to have you at my side. These virtues, among others, were the ones that made me notice you, brought me closer to you and made me love you as I've never loved anyone. Now, with a mature love, an awareness of the future and an unquenchable desire to spend the rest of my life with you.

I chose the path that I wanted to follow and knew the risks and why I was doing it. I imposed this reality upon you without your knowing or expressing an opinion about what I was doing and what I was dedicating my life to. The current situation has demanded from you personal growth, strength and sacrifice that I never doubted you would be prepared for. You have demonstrated it and even continue demonstrating day by day with your resistance and support, which encourage me. I appreciate them so much.

Listening to your voice on the phone is like receiving one of your caresses that I miss so much and that I know we'll have time to share in the years to come.

A kiss on the lips, I whisper in your ear: I love you very much.

For Fernando
[excerpts]
[undated]
Havana

Fernan,

...it doesn't matter how long we have to wait, the truth will come out... I continue to wait for you with the same love as always — you know I'm a dreamer and haven't stopped being one — so I wait for our bright future, and I'll keep on making plans. Don't worry about me, take good care of yourself, and keep loving me a lot, since it's love that keeps us firm and strong.

For Rosa
[excerpts]
[undated]
Oxford, Wisconsin

Rosa,

It doesn't matter how long we have to wait or the influence that time may have on us physically. When the time comes for us to be together again, I will be there, beside you, so that you don't miss me ever again, either in the mornings or in the nights. I'll be there every morning to tell you how beautiful you look in your work uniform and every night, to say it again. All this time will be left behind like a distant memory and we will tell each other stories by the sea, hand in hand.

For Fernando
[excerpts]
August 14, 2002
Havana

Fernan,

...today I'm really trying harder than ever to follow your example — I don't know if I'll be able to, but I swear I'm trying, since you've made me a better person... Maybe I never valued the importance of what I received, believing that it was due to me, but today I know the price of each minute of tranquility we have. Forgive me if I was ever lazy, and didn't value this, demanding more attention from you. You deserve all my love and you know that you have it. Not a single day goes by that I don't dedicate my best thoughts to you, hoping they'll reach your soul... Don't worry about me, I'm confident and wait for you with all my love.

For Rosa
[excerpts]
September 30, 2002
Oxford, Wisconsin

My Rosa,

I don't want you to follow my example because I am no better than you. I want us to take our steps together, I want us to leave just one footprint, ours, just one. Not mine or yours, but ours. Only one.

For Rosa
[undated]
Oxford, Wisconsin

I see you walking toward me,
And I can't take my eyes off you.
It's not only your body approaching. It's more than that.
With you comes spring after a long winter.
And when you are with me, worries disappear. Only tenderness
remains.
I lose myself in the blue of your eyes and I am happy. I dream.
Through your eyes, I see the future. Without them, there is none.
I take your hand, stare into your face,
And find myself. I am and I am not.
A little bit of me is gone, as I redefine myself through you.
I walk your steps, dream your dreams, quench my thirst with
your drink.
Here's my heart. When I wake up I want to be by your side.

(I can hardly call this poetry, it doesn't even have a title. Just ideas
that came to me, one after the other.)

For Rosa
[excerpts]
[undated]
Oxford, Wisconsin

I have a close-up of you that Bill took and it really hurts me to have to part with it. However, after having it for months in the mural of my cell I want you to have it and preserve it. It is too big so it doesn't fit my album and I wouldn't want it to get lost in any movement or "hole." I separate from this picture with the same sadness that I separate from you at the end of our limited visits. It accompanied me for months in my cell. Any angle I looked at it, it seemed as if you were staring at me. Many times, in the solitude of my cell, I found myself looking at that photo and having an imaginary dialogue with you, one of those that we so frequently had and I miss like you cannot imagine.

Fernando can only have a small album of photos in his cell. Those are the rules. When he receives new ones, he has to get rid of the others and obey the rules. He always sends them back home for us to keep. He is also afraid all the time that he might lose everything if he is put in the "hole" or if he is transferred to another prison. That is why he sent me that picture he likes so much which was taken by Bill, an American friend who is involved in the fight for the liberation of the Cuban Five. Bill was in Havana more than a year ago.

For Rosa
[undated]
Oxford, Wisconsin

Love,

I know that it's been two years since you moved to the new apartment, so it's old news for you, but try to put yourself in my place: I don't know anything about that change and I'd like to know so much. What was it like to move? How did you fix up the place? What's the neighborhood like? How are you managing with the new household responsibilities? The same with your work. When we talked, you mentioned that you were promoted — yet, in your letters you don't go into any detail. I'd like to know what your new job consists of, if you like it, if you're satisfied, if you have possibilities to develop, what changes you've had to make in your routine, how you're managing with the work and the house. Since I'm not a poet, I've chosen a poem by Mario Benedetti (I know he's a favorite of yours) to share with you. It's included in the book *Inventory*, which I told you about in my last letter, and it's called "Still." Be confident in victory and keep your optimism. I'm taking care of myself and I'm prepared for anything. With this letter I send you all my love and a big kiss. I love you,

Fernando

I was studying the economics of cooperation at a technical school in Havana. I was friends with Martha, Fernando's sister, and I told her that I was having problems with subjects like political economy and philosophy. So she introduced me to her brother to help me. Fernando had a degree in international economic relations, and he was very patient with me. We were neighbors, and things had never gone beyond a simple hello. But from then on, we were closer. Of course, I felt attracted to him, but I never thought a relationship possible... He enthusiastically helped me with my homework, and then with my thesis. We started going to the movies and theater together. We borrowed books from each other. But neither one of us took the initiative. Neither of us dared to go beyond the threshold of a friendship that was becoming more and more complicated. In the process, he just about destroyed my neighbor's jealously guarded bushes of jasmine and roses. He would steal the flowers for me, with whatever excuse. And then one day the inevitable happened.

For Rosa
November 9, 2002
Oxford, Wisconsin

My *flaca,*

Maybe this letter will be a little bit different from the others because I won't be telling you about me or updating you on the latest developments here, or talking about what I've been reading, or what I think.

What I want is to try to make you see and feel the immense love I have for you, and how much I value your tender company, your love and understanding, intelligence and sweetness, your patience and attentions. That is, just how important you are to me, and how I'm taking very good care of the love I'm keeping for you, so I can give it to you, and so you can make it grow and deepen with your everyday actions that demonstrate that my heart wasn't wrong when it gave itself to you so completely.

You've shown me feelings that I'd never known or experienced. Little by little, as the years went by and for a long time now, you entered through the cracks in the protective armor I'd involuntarily built around me.

With that love you warmed my heart as only you know how to do, and gave new meaning — until then unknown to me — to what it is to love and be a couple.

Today, from such a distance and under such extraordinary conditions, you've kept that warmth, and you keep on taking care of our love, our relationship and our future like someone who is taking care of what is most precious to them.

And that makes me admire and love you more every day, confident that the happiness we've had would die of envy seeing the happiness that we'll have in the future...

And that's how I love you, always present, with your encouragement so near, always with your sweet words and your strong spirit, always with that warmth that you've given to my heart and the happiness that you make me feel. And that's how I'll always have you.

I love you,
Fernando

For Rosa
[postcard]
December 25, 2002
Oxford, Wisconsin

My love,
Although today we are not together physically, I would like this to be a day of happiness for you.

The courage, moral strength and dignity you show every day; your ability to resist and to fight, confident in the future of love and happiness that awaits us; all that makes me feel so proud of you and at the same time enriches more and more my list of reasons why I love you.

Your love and affection are always with me and, in the most difficult and cold moments, they make my heart warm and help me stand up for the fight.

Do not despair. The future is ours and we will enjoy it with the greatest satisfaction of all, which is when you feel that you have done your duty, that your dignity is intact and your love strengthened. I wish you a happy birthday and I send you all my love, which is immense, and a warm kiss on your delicate lips.

Happy Birthday!

With love,

Fernando

For Rosa

[excerpts]

January 28, 2003

Oxford, Wisconsin

Today I didn't see you, and since it's easy to get used to good things, you can't imagine how much I miss you. I can't wait til Friday, to see you again, look into your eyes and spend the whole day with your warm hand in mine.

The rose in this drawing should have had colors, but you know what it's like here — there aren't any. I hope you like it as it is, and that it's enough to substitute a garden rose as my gift for you.

For Fernando

[excerpts]

[undated]

Havana

Fernan,

Although it may seem incredible, I'm responding to a letter you wrote almost a month ago, but as you say, these things are inevitable circumstances we have to deal with. Not to worry, I've learned to have a little patience and not to become so desperate at the delays in correspondence. And when your letters arrive, so beautiful and filled with such love, they sweep away all the anxiety produced by the waiting... Every letter of yours is something I need, and each one gives me support... (Ah, and tell me about the bonsai).

For Rosa
[excerpts]
[March 2003]
Oxford, Wisconsin

Nelson told me about his bonsai tree. He thought it appropriate that we could do the project together, as friends, and he's begun to trim the plant. He said it's doing well. I already told him that under these circumstances, there's not much I can do to contribute. I have no books on bonsai, so I can't help him with instructions. I had sent him some notes on how and where to trim the plant, and what shape to give it. If everything works out, the plant will look like it's growing over a stone. He's already working on it. I hope the jailers haven't thrown away my books. In Cuba, I won't fill our house with plants, but I'd like to have at least one decent bonsai.

He sent this letter from the "hole," the last time they put the Five in there, each in their respective prisons. It was in March 2003, when they were preparing the documents with their attorneys for the appeal. He tells me about the books that Nelson, a man who lives in Madison, had sent him through the mail, and in which he read how to create a bonsai tree. They kept up a warm correspondence and agreed on growing a bonsai they would dedicate to peace and friendship. As Fernan cannot grow plants in prison, he would give advice to Nelson, following the instructions in the books, and his friend would take care of the little tree. However, when they put Fernando in the "hole," they did not give him his things. He was afraid

that he would lose his few belongings, including this book, should the
confinement extend as long as he had been told: at least a year.

For Rosa
[excerpts]
March 10, 2003
Oxford, Wisconsin

To hatred, we have to respond with love: love for Cuba, love for our
people, love for Fidel... That love should and will be reflected in
more love between us. The limitations don't matter. Our love will
grow and we'll become stronger. Again I have to tell you: "Don't
become desperate." Nothing they do or try to do is going to prevent
truth and justice from winning out. The future is ours and we'll
enjoy what they've stolen from us.

For Rosa
[excerpts]
[undated]
Oxford, Wisconsin

Flaca,
    ...you were telling me over the phone that you were waiting for
my thoughts on what to hang on the walls. Being so far away, it's
difficult to be very precise, but I guess one good option would be
some lithographs like the ones the artisans sell. I'm glad to hear that
your family visits you on Sundays, and that Ale [Rosa's nephew]
sometimes stays over on Saturday. That means you're not so alone.
Please give my regards to all of them, including the doctor, her mother
and stepfather. Now that I mention Laura [his niece] I have to say
that her letter was a big surprise for me. The things she says and

how she says them really moved me, and show that she's a teenager who's maturing, and I was amazed at the knack she had for expressing her feelings.

Sometimes I think people have a wrong image of Fernando, as if he were a little lead soldier, a perfect hero. They take him out of reality, out of context. But you don't fall in love with a man because he's a hero. Fernando is very easy to live with — he's very affectionate, and is always thinking of little things, little ways to show it. For instance, sometimes he would be watching television, and he'd stop and come over and give me a kiss, pulling me over to sit with him. He loved going out together on the weekends, which of course are the days when you have the most housework — doing the washing, for one, the chore I like the least. So if there were a lot of clothes in the laundry, he'd just pitch in and start washing, too, to finish that much faster so we could go out. He's no lead soldier, someone to keep in a glass showcase. He is a human being like any other — but maybe more tender than anyone I know.

For Rosa
[excerpts]
September 14, 2003
Oxford, Wisconsin

My love,

You can't imagine how much I miss you. You are on my mind all day long and in everything I do. And, in my dreams! Rare is the night you're not with me there. One way or another, you're my permanent company. Your joyful spirit and your enthusiasm for our struggle is a source of inspiration for me, too.

I can't have you in my arms now, but you're with me in a thousand ways. No one can take that away from me. I spend a lot of time sitting at the desk in my cell writing or studying and, since I have a picture of you in front of me on the wall, every time I glance up your blue eyes are there for me. I can feel your look as I can feel your hands, with that tenderness of yours that gives me so much pleasure, which I'm going to reclaim the moment I see you again. I can't stop loving you. How could I?

For Rosa
[postcard]
December 25, 2003
Oxford, Wisconsin

My love,

Receive with this postcard all my love and affection on your birthday. I hope that, in spite of the circumstances, it will be a happy day for you. Remember that our sacrifice of today will become our joy and happiness of tomorrow. I kiss you with love and wish you from the bottom of my heart:

Happy Birthday!
I love you,
Fernando

For Rosa
[excerpts]
December 2003
Oxford, Wisconsin

My *flaca*,

As the years pass for us in U.S. prisons, reality makes us assimilate and accept our circumstances as part of a necessary sacrifice. But that doesn't mean it isn't painful. Guided by revolutionary consciousness, the absolute conviction that truth is on our side, and the certainty that we are defending a just cause, we put the pain into perspective, and learn to accept reality and live with it.

One of the most painful aspects for us is the children we had planned to have — children that time has decided we will never have. As the years go by, and the biological clocks advance, the separation imposed on us has forced us to transform our vision of a family into one without children, though still full of love.

So in our house, love will have to substitute for a baby's laughter, the constant attention to raising our absent children, and the pleasure and satisfaction of watching them grow up as human beings committed to all that is noble and just. Surely my case isn't unique. Nevertheless, what distinguishes our pain is that it is provoked by a colossal injustice...

I AM HERE, ALWAYS LOVING ALL OF YOU

Ramón Labañino Salazar

Elizabeth Palmeiro

Ramón and I were married on June 2, 1990. On August 9, 1992, our first daughter Laura — who is the image of her father — was born. Four years later, our second treasure, Lizbeth, was born. Ailí, Ramón's oldest daughter, is from his first marriage. He calls us his four women.

It was very difficult to explain to them that their father had been arrested in Miami. He was accused of conspiracy to commit espionage, of having false documentation and of being a non-registered Cuban agent in the United States. It is a very weird feeling that such strange words all of a sudden control our lives. I needed a language that our daughters, from the innocence of their infancy, could easily understand. The biggest challenge was with Laura because she has always been the closest to her father. Ramón calls her his little princess. I felt better with Lizbeth because, being the youngest, I knew she would not ask questions that are difficult to answer. Ailí, who was 13, understood everything better than her sisters.

It was in June 2001. I had recently had my appendix taken out and I asked Laurita to lay by my side. I explained to her as best I could that since September 1998 Ramón had been arrested and that they were accusing him of being a spy and of endangering U.S. national security. I told her that it was not true, that her father was in prison because he was a patriot who had defended his people from terrorist attacks and that he had not harmed anyone. I said that her father was in prison for defending us all from death. I also explained that he was tried and convicted in Miami and sentenced to life. Laura began to cry. Not to make her feel worse, I held my tears.

Ramón's letters somehow began to fill the emptiness that his absence had created. For the last five years, our family life has been marked by the arbitrariness and psychological blackmail that Ramón and his four compañeros have suffered. The first letter that we received from him was

dated December 27, 2000 — 25 months after the Five had been imprisoned.
It was not until April 2002 that our family was together again, after almost
four years of imprisonment.

For Elizabeth
[excerpts]
December 27, 2000
Miami FDC

My beloved wife, my dear family,

I'm taking this opportunity, after a "long" period of silence, to
send each of you my unlimited love and to tell you how I long to see
you again. In fact, I've never been far from you — you've always
been at my side throughout these more than two years, and your
presence — those of you who remain and those who have passed
away — is my best ally every moment of my life.

To my daughters, who are always with me, you can't imagine
how much I think of you, of your laughter and fancies, your games
and mischief, but above all, of that little-girl love you've always
given me. A kiss and daddy's love to each of you.

I await your needed "long" letters and photos of everyone — but
most of all of you and my daughters, and all of my friends and
family. I know that many things must have happened during all
this time, so I hope you'll bring me up-to-date on everything. I hope
you'll be able to receive a gift from me for the new year, the end of the
millennium, since I've begun the process of adding your number to
the list of phone numbers I can call, and hope that in roughly a week
I'll be able to call home. My plan is to call on Saturdays between
eight and 10 in the morning — I hope I'll be able to before 2001. Calls
are very expensive and I don't have much money now, so let's see
how I can distribute them best. We'll only have 15 minutes, which
we'll need to make the most of. I hope you'll be able to have everybody

on hand — or at least a big part of the family — so I can talk with
everybody, but first with you and my daughters. You don't know
how I long for that day, when I can hear your voice and the voices of
my girls. It will seem like a "dream." So, get ready...

As to everything else, don't worry, it will all come to light and the
"truth will set us free" as one of the great geniuses of all times once
said.

Papo, daddy

For Ramón
December 2000
Havana

Daddy Ramón,
I will write you a poem, which I hope you like.

Why do they imprison?

Americans, you don't reason
that it was done for no good reason.
For goodness' sake alive,
release the five.

[Laurita]

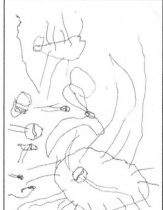

**Drawing by Lizbeth for Ramón
(at three years old)**

For Elizabeth
[excerpts]
January, 2001
Miami FDC

My dear wife,

I want to tell you that in the most difficult moments, in the depths of solitude, when we missed the simple sound of a human voice (and were even afraid to lose communication altogether, longing to hear any word, just one, in any language spoken by anyone), I always, always have had you with me. You, your smile, and our remarkable love story. In those dire times you have always been at my side. My mother was also with me. All of you were there — my daughters, my loved ones, my friends, and first of all, our beloved homeland, to which we all owe our lives.

Everything started on September 12, 1998, at about 5:30 a.m. at home, when we were detained and taken to FBI headquarters in Miami for a "persuasive" interview, where they asked us to collaborate and betray our country with promises offered in return. Obviously I had nothing to say, and after they were sure they were getting nowhere, they put us in a car and took us to the Federal Detention Center in downtown Miami, where we've been all this time.

I'd like you to take a picture of my four women: you and our three daughters, all fixed up, with hair combed and bangs. That way I can better look at my treasures.

[Ramón]

For Ramón
[excerpts]
January 4, 2001
Havana

Ramón, my love,

The first thing I want you to receive in these first lines after more than two years is all my love for you, all your daughters' love. We've never forgotten you. We live as if you were here with us... I've had a lot of time to go over each day we've known each other, convinced that you are the man of my life — and this gives me strength to face whatever is to come. I won't say it hasn't been hard, very hard, but I've had the support of a lot of people who love me and have shared my lonely efforts with our daughters, trying to make them happy. One day, our daughters will be proud of the love of their parents... I love you so very, very, very much,

Your Eli

For Elizabeth
[excerpts]
January, 2001
Miami FDC

For Eli,

It's my role as a father to be up-to-date and always to be teaching — even at a distance. So I'm sending a drawing to Lizbeth, my little one who can't read yet, with some ideas and tasks for you to read to her. I'd like you to hang this drawing over her bed: it's meant to be a serious duckling, questioning whether she's done her daily chores (the list underneath). That way, she'll always see it, so that she'll remember her daddy and at the same time remember her daily responsibilities, and the drawings and notes will give her encouragement.

[Ramón]

For Laurita
[undated]
Miami FDC

Poem of Love to My Daughter

Lovely pretty Chinese eyes
Adored smile of mine
Uniting as if they were two lilies
Reason, love and poetry
Alike is she to her daddy
You are my little daughter.

Dad loves you so much...

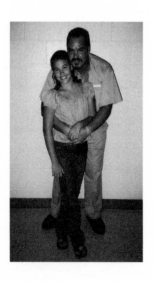

For Elizabeth
[excerpts]
January, 2001
Miami FDC

Laurita is charming, beautiful and very big. It's not just me, everyone here says she's the spitting image of me, which makes me very proud and happy. I can't tell you how much I love and miss her — since we had more time together with her, and you know how sensitive and affectionate she is with me, her presence is something I miss and long for. Tell her how much I love her — that I live for her, just as I do for you, for all my daughters, all my loved ones.

[Ramón]

For Ramón
January 4, 2001
Havana

Dear dad,

Happy new year! — that's from me and my little sister. As you can see, I can write and read correctly. I have also learned to add and subtract, and also to multiply and divide, though I don't know all the tables yet. But at least I have a lot of little stars on my homework notebook. When I finished second grade, I got an award, since I got Excellent on all my exams.

I tell you I take care of my little sister and play with her, so mommy can do the housework. When I get out of school, I go to the day care center to stay with her until mommy finishes work and picks us up.

Well, daddy, I send you lots of kisses from me and my little sister. I miss you and love you very much.

Love,

Your daughter Laurita xxxxxx! A kiss

For Laura
January 29, 2001
Miami FDC

Laura, my little princess,

I hope you like this short story. Like every story, it has a message and a lesson I hope you'll learn: how important kindness is, graciousness (like yours) and helping people who need your help. The Princess Dayra (like you), shows how important it is to learn how to read and write and study hard, since that helped her to find the unicorn, and save it so it could go back to its mother.

It shows how important it is to know how to read, to learn and be a good student, just as you are and should always be. I hope you like this story. The drawings are for you to color. In your letters, be sure to tell me what you think of the stories, and if you want me to send you more, and which ones.

This is just a sampling of how much I love and miss you...

Kisses,

Daddy

For Ramón
[undated]
Havana

Daddy, I went to grandma's house and had a great time riding a bike and jumping rope during the school break. Daddy, I got an award for being such a good student, and I'll mail the certificate to you. I called mommy to tell her and she was very happy. I have a wish for my sister's birthday — that you call us, to tell her happy birthday. That's my biggest wish. Bye-bye, daddy. Kisses xxxxxx

Laurita

For Laura
[excerpts]
February 3, 2001
Miami FDC

Laurita, my beloved, precious daughter,

...I want to explain the little present I'm sending you here: it's my first 10 stamps, and I send them to you as a prize for your wonderful school grades, for being such a good student and well-behaved daughter, and above all for all the letters you've sent to me all this time, and for all the kisses and love you've sent with them. So, here are my 10 stamps for you, the highest award for being the one who has sent me the most letters, drawings, kisses and poems.

Stamp collecting is really fascinating. Stamps are works of art kept in collections according to themes, and you can also exchange them with your friends. People who collect stamps are called philatelists or stamp collectors. As you can see, the stamps are colorful and are made all over the world. There are many ways of collecting: you can collect the stamps you receive, or exchange them with other collectors, or buy them, etc.

A good collection can be very valuable, worth a lot of money, but mostly valuable in terms of the historical and artistic value of the stamps. You can also collect stamps — from the letters you receive, from the letters your grandma gets from your uncle, or the ones that your friends and schoolmates receive. Really, all stamps are valuable... Don't ever throw a stamp away, since you can always exchange it for another one you want.

Read this part about the stamps to your sisters Ailí and Lizbeth, so they can learn about them, too. I'm also sending some stamps for them because they won them. Write me and tell me about the stamps, if you liked them, and what you're doing with them.

Well, my precious one, I love you very, very much. And I'm sending you a big kiss, just like the ones you send me in your letters. I miss you very much. Remember that daddy loves you.

Your daddy, Ramón

For Ramón
February 4, 2001
Havana

Daddy,

My sister was behaving herself, but not anymore. First, she wants to rip my calendar up. She takes all my things and loses them. I'll tell you what she lost, she lost two of my new pencils when I was at grandma's house.

I'm sweating, and I already had my bath. I'm sweaty and tired because I spent the entire afternoon tidying up. Mommy was very happy and I know you are, too, because you called us on the phone. Well, daddy, here's a big kiss from,

Your little daughter Laurita
It's 6:20 p.m. here now.

For Ramón
[excerpts]
February 5, 2001
Havana

Papo,

Today I put Laurita's letters in order. As you can see, they're very original and spontaneous. She wrote them all by herself, in her own way. I tried to correct her handwriting, because she started on the first line and finished the idea almost at the end of the page, but she wouldn't let me... We're all fine, waiting to come together and celebrate your return in a big way. The girls and I will always look forward to that day, but in the meantime, my priority is to raise them safe and sound, strong, healthy and well educated, but above all, worthy of their father. So that when they're old enough to look back and assess this time, they'll do it with pride in you and your life. So that their love for their father will fill their lives, and they'll see you as I do: honorable and brave. That's how I began to love you, and I've adapted the life of my daughters to that love. I want you to be able to see that when you're here with us again. I love you,

Eli

For Ramón
[excerpts]
March 10, 2001
Havana

I'm doing fine at school, and even won a few days camping at the lake. We had a lot of fun, we went to the beach and the disco (even though you know I'm not a great dancer). I went to Lizbeth's birthday party. There were only a few people there, but we had a great time. Laura ate everything she wanted (she is a little bit fat). She studies very hard, she likes to read and send you lots of letters. I love you,

Ailí

For Ramón
May 22, 2001
Havana

Dear dad,

   I wish you a very, very happy birthday and a very happy Father's Day. Also, tell your *compañeros* that I wish them a happy Father's Day, too. I love you like I love my palm tree and I love my flag. They are prettier now.

> I got sick with L
> Which I got from O
> And Doctor V
> Prescribed me an E.

I want to tell you that your wife is beautiful and she loves you as much as you love her, and I love you both so much. My little sister loves you as much as I do. Love,
   Laurita

For Laura
May 2001
Miami FDC

Dear Laurita, my sweet child,

   Every day I think and dream of you, of our things together, only yours and mine, our thousands of games and times of fun, our strolls and the tricks we played on each other, our love, yours and mine. I make plans, many plans, for when I go home, since I want to take you everywhere with me, to cities and mountains, to the sky and the clouds, and we'll go swimming in all the rivers and beaches in Cuba, and we'll explore every inch of our beloved island together, always together.

Dad Ramón

For Ramón
[undated]
Havana

Dear dad,

I miss you very much. As for me, school is going well, and I've been getting good grades on all my exams, and I still have to take tests in chemistry, English and math. Eli says that if we put a mustache on Laura, she'd be a perfect copy of you, and both of them, Lizbeth too, have Chinese eyes like yours. Well, dad, receive a big kiss — the size of the sea — from your Ailí Labañino (that's how my teachers and classmates call me, which makes me think of you, and makes me very happy).

For Ailí
[excerpts]
May 31, 2001
Miami FDC

Precious daughter,

I want to congratulate you for the good grades you got at school and for being a good student and participating in all the activities. I just ask you to continue being like that, doing your best so you can study at a university and be a woman with a great and wonderful future. I'm sure it will be so. Tell me in detail how your travel for the competition was, where you stayed, what you did, which competition you participated in, how you felt, how were your friends... in short, tell me about everything and in details. And also, about future plans.

Little daughter, next year you'll be 15, and I'll try to make it the most wonderful birthday of your life. Tell me how you're planning to celebrate, what you would wish to do, what plans your mother has, all the ideas you've come up with. Precious one, since you're becoming a young woman, I think it's a good time to talk about more mature and serious topics. Today I want to talk with you about love, but only to give you some advice.

Love is the purest and most profound feeling that a person has for others (fathers, mothers, friends, sons, daughters, family, wives, husbands, boyfriends, etc.) or for things (homelands, the earth, flags, ideas, etc.).

Love is beautiful, generous, unselfish, and it can sometimes be painful, when someone hurts you or doesn't love you back.

But you have to cultivate love, take care of it, nurture it and make it grow — and never forget that it is there. Love is a rose that needs constant watering, or it withers and dies. How do you nurture love? With little things, and always with tenderness. Never stop giving your mother a good morning kiss, or saying "I love you," a hug, a caress, a phone call if you're far away, a poem, a song dedicated to her, a little gift, a flower...

There are little things you can't forget, no matter where you are, no matter what you're doing...

[Ramón]

For Lizbeth
[excerpts]
May 31, 2001
Miami FDC

My playful little girl,

...you don't know how much daddy misses you and how much I want to see you to hug you and be together always, never to part.

You are very pretty in the pictures from your little friend Ivette's birthday party. I like your little face and your lovely hair.

Mommy says you're behaving yourself, and you're very affectionate with her. You know that I'm your daddy. Your mommy and I made you with a lot of love and we were very happy to bring you to live with us. So, mommy loves you and your daddy loves you, too, and always will.

It was also us, Mommy Elizabeth and Daddy Ramón, who brought you together with your sisters Laurita and Ailí so that you could all be happy and play a lot. That's why you should love your sisters, take care of them and listen to them, because they're older than you and they look after you.

When Daddy Ramón (that's me), when I come back we are going to play a lot and have a lot of fun. That's why you have to be a good girl and take care of yourself.

Sending you a big hug and all my love,

Daddy Ramón

Ailí and Laura regularly write to Ramón, and little Lizbeth — who is learning to write — sends him her drawings. She met her father for the first time in prison, when she was five and a half. From asking over and over to have her father's letters read to her, she has memorized some of them. She likes when Ramón calls her "my little mischievous one." Ramón desperately attempts to maintain a close relationship with his daughters by every means available to him. He writes them letters, poems. He sends them drawings and postcards. He asks me and the girls to recount the smallest details of our daily lives.

For Ramón
[undated]
Havana

Dear daddy,

I miss you a lot and I would like you to come back so that mommy can show you my good grades. Lizbeth is a little fat — now she's eating the ham and cheese off the spaghetti. Well, daddy, good-bye. This is my latest letter. Daddy. Daddy. Daddy Ramón.

[Laurita]

For Laura
[excerpts]
May 31, 2001
Miami FDC

My Laurita, my little princess,

A big kiss, a big one... and all my love to you, my daughter. I just finished looking at your pictures of Ivette's birthday party and I loved them. You look very pretty and slim. I realized that you are growing fast and, to my satisfaction, you look more and more like me. So, you're like my reflection.

I liked your stamps of Cuban martyrs and patriots. I want you to keep that collection apart, a page just for them. I have some here for you that I'll send you soon.

I also like your poems and especially the one about love for your daddy. Thank you, my little girl.

Laury, don't forget to follow my advice about diet and food that I sent in the drawing. I want you to be very pretty and healthy, so we can all go out together when I get home, everywhere — to parks, discos, the Morro Castle — so take good care of yourselves for daddy.

Every day when you wake up, give mommy a kiss and tell her how much you and I love her. Remember that daddy is always thinking of you and that he loves you very much…

I love you,

Daddy Ramón

For Ramón

[undated]

Havana

Daddy, this is my letter for you. Dear daddy. This is my latest letter. I hope you like it like the others. I was going to ask you when you're coming back, but mommy told me not to because it would make you sad.

Laurita

For His Daughters
[excerpts]
July 11, 2001
Miami FDC

My beloved little daughters,

I know this is a time of a lot of emotion, happiness and surprise that you may never have imagined. Today, you're learning who your father really is and also learning about those four brothers of mine who are with me, about our real lives and what we did to save your dreams and safeguard the dreams of our people… That's why we left one day, and are far away from our loved ones.

Sometimes, the more you love someone, the faster you have to go away to save that person's life and even their dreams.

You're learning things that I would have liked to tell you someday in person, but that moment didn't come. Anyway, I'm happy that the very people we defend tell you these things rather than me. I could never have told you my life story in so much detail and with so much love, like you are seeing on television and in the rallies, and hearing from my *compañeros*, and even from our dear *comandante*. I know that it will help you to understand everything better.

Now you can understand why daddy couldn't be with you longer, or share all the happy times with you like other fathers do with their children. For that, I'm very sorry.

For that, and for my absences, because I couldn't be at mommy's side during her pregnancy, because I couldn't see you be born, because I couldn't be there when you opened your precious eyes for the first time, or to change your diapers, or help you to take your first steps or clean up your "pee-pee" and "poo," or see your first smile or hear your first words — the first "daddy," "mommy" or "I love you." For not taking care of you when you were sick or playing with you all the games fathers love to play with their children, not even being able to teach you your first vowels or read you your first book, and for the fact that my littlest one barely knows me. For all that, I apologize, my beloved daughters.

But I want you to know that I had to leave because of my love for you and everyone. That wherever I have been and wherever I will be, you have been and will always be with me.

Be strong, very strong to face whatever life brings with a smile. Don't be afraid for me, I am well and I am strong, especially now that you are with me like my people and the dignity of the world. I'll come back, never doubt that, as soon as I can, because I miss you very much. When I come home, we'll make up for all my absences, and rebuild all the hopes and dreams that have been waiting for us... Good-bye!

Daddy Ramón

From Ramón's Diary
[excerpts]
[undated]
Miami FDC

One day I found myself in my room listening as usual to the program "Haciendo Radio" (Making Radio) on Rebel Radio[6] — it was 6:55 a.m., the time they air greetings to us from people back home. Just then, another "tenant," a Cuban, came to get me for the workout we'd scheduled. I asked him not to interrupt yet, and when he asked why, I told him to tune his radio to Rebel Radio. By chance, the day was the first day of school for the 2001-02 school year, and my two eldest daughters were being interviewed, their emotions showing through with the lovely words they dedicated to me. I was concen-

---

6. Broadcasting from 9600 KHz, 31m for Central America and 11,655 KHz, 25m for the Caribbean.

trating so much that I hardly noticed the fellow discreetly dabbing away the tears. When the program ended, he left without a word. Almost an hour later he returned with a piece of paper with words he had written for my daughters and me.

For Ramón
December 13, 2001
Havana

Thursday, 3:30 p.m.
  Dear and beloved daddy,
  Daddy, in this letter I can't write the song "The Man I Love," so I'll write a poem.

The Four

  Don't count to three, count to four
  Because if you count to three, three will be in the family:
  Mommy, girl and little baby
  But you forget something if you count
  To three. And so, who is missing?
  Daddy.

Daddy, did you like the poem I wrote?

Little Dove by the Beach

  On the seashore
  A dove is singing
  Singing sweetly
  Weeping sadly

Singing sweetly
The white dove.
The young pigeons fly off
And leave her alone.

Ciao, Daddy Ramón. I love you,
   Laurita

For Elizabeth
[excerpts]
July 18, 2002
Beaumont, Texas

I always dreamed of having a son. You know that. I think anybody who knows me knows it, too. For me, it's like realizing a dream, a hope or joy, the same joy you make me feel every day since that moment your lips and your soul said that endless "yes." Such is the enormity of my dream of a "little prince."

And you know that it's not for lack of affection or fatherly love, because I have the tremendous good fortune of having my three little princesses, who I love dearly and who make me feel fulfilled. I am a completely happy and fortunate father having you and my three little princesses, for everything we are and have been.

I'd say, though, that this is something else, deeper — perhaps the desire of having a son in my arms, of kissing his bare little feet, of bathing him and taking care of him every second, of teaching him how to walk, to read, to write, to play and practice all the sports I know, and all the others which, because of my work, I never could practice myself. I love you,
   Papo

For His Daughters
[autographed picture]
May 27, 2002
Beaumont, Texas

I feel tenderness and pride… My daughters are my treasure, my love.
The first lesson of those dreams is that there is no anger or discour-
agement that our strength can't topple. Here I am with my dreams,
always in victory, loving you. With all my love,
    Papo, Daddy, Ramón

I traveled with our daughters for a family visit to the federal prison of
Beaumont, Texas. Until then, we had received his letters with regularity,
first from Miami FDC and then from Beaumont USP.

He never complained or transmitted the slightest sign of suffering. In his letters he always expressed his desire to be with his daughters. I know that Ramón had been locked down at least on three occasions – for 17 months after his arrest, for 48 days after he made public a message to the U.S. people, and for 31 days on the eve of the appeal process before the 11th Circuit Court of Appeals of Atlanta. But love can create ties that need no words. Ramón and I, from the distance and in spite of the bars and walls, have an unspoken pact to protect the children from anything that could harm them.

For Ailí
[excerpts]
November 30, 2002
Beaumont, Texas

For Ailí from her daddy,
Today you turn 15. Who would have thought it! How time flies!
It seems just yesterday I had you in my arms for the first time, discovering every inch of your tiny body, cuddling and kissing you as delicately as sunlight. And now you're a young woman: beautiful, slender, tall, elegant, my daughter... You were born on a particularly beautiful day. The sun shone outside in the middle of a morning cool and warm at the same time, so typical of our beautiful island in November. I was inside, in the waiting room of the Maternidad Obrera Hospital, uneasy, nervous, joyful, not knowing what to do. I'd talked to every doctor and nurse in the hospital, and I don't think that there was anyone who didn't know of your imminent arrival.
[Ramón]

For Lizbeth
February 23, 2003
Beaumont, Texas

For Lizbeth, on reaching her 5th birthday

To my pretty little princess
To the youngest of all my joys
Today daddy gives you irises
Which are roses of your little smile.

For Ailí

August 15, 2003

Beaumont, Texas

To my beloved daughter Ailí

I have many reasons
To love you like I do
For your silence-colored eyes
For the honey pink in your lips
For your blond curls
And the fragrance you leave behind.
I have many reasons to love you like I do
But of all the reasons, my favorite
Is being your father
Your creator
Your sovereign
You will never find
Another who loves you
Like I do
I love you.

For Ramón

[excerpts]

November 8, 2003

Havana

Dear daddy,

I hope you're not doing too many exercises that can affect your leg (I know you're just a little bit "stubborn").

This school year is a bit difficult (like all sophomore years). I have new classes and although the professors try hard, they don't explain things well enough. We have to study a lot to be able "to understand at least something" (without books in the field, and the few there are we share among a lot of students). In English, we're translating (from English to Spanish) computer science texts (fairly complicated ones) and so far I don't know one student I can study with who has a technical dictionary.

Every Saturday, I go into the office with Eli to put the poems together. Today, I started to put together a power-point show, where I insert one of your poems with one of the pictures we took when we visited you. I finished 10 slides today, I hope you like them... I don't want to talk about Osmel (a friend of mine) in this letter, because my mind is on my worries about architecture homework. But I promise I will in my next letter.

Big kisses for a big daddy from his "littlest daughter,"

Ailicita

From time to time Ramón is able to call home, and Laura and Ailí even manage to share small secrets with him. They are older, and maintain a more intense dialogue with their father. But the littlest one doesn't understand yet why her father isn't home. The last time Ramón called home she didn't want to speak to him. "If he wants to tell me something, he should come here!" she shouted at me, and broke into tears.

Drawing by Lizbeth for her father[1]

For His Daughters
[undated]
Beaumont, Texas

To my daughters

I gave you life,
I sprinkled your love with dew,
glorified your soul in mine,
and grew from your challenges...

My life turned into three,
three my wishes and destinies,
three my grateful happiness,
three my plans and fortunes.

For you, I would exist,
wherever I am and reside,
as all my love goes only to you,
I exist only in you.

I may be far away today
and so can't share your joys
but know that wherever I am
I love you all.
Wherever I am,
it's for you
I live!

---

1. The drawing opposite represents Lizbeth's mother, her sisters and herself, carrying a square (the ink mark stamped on her hand, like all visitors, in order to enter the prison).

For Elizabeth
[excerpts]
[undated]
Beaumont, Texas

All the pictures you send me make me very happy, and some make me nostalgic (especially those of my mother), but without a doubt it's infinite joy I feel to see what a lovely family I've created, thanks to you, my love. I made a selection of the pictures and I've hung the best ones (it was hard to choose) on the wall in my cell. Everybody has something to say about them. So, that's why I'm asking you to send me more, especially the most recent ones, to see how you are, and the girls in particular.

Eli, keep showing the girls pictures of me, videos, letters, poems, anything of mine. Especially to Lizbeth, who knows me the least. Talk to them about me all the time, about Dad Ramón, who loves them and misses them...

For Ramón
June 2004
Havana

Why?

Why is my love for you
so big?
Perhaps because you created me,
I don't think so.
Why when I leave you
is the world not the same?
Perhaps it's a silliness of mine,
I don't think so.
Why isn't there in the world
someone better than you?
Now I know why,
because my love isn't like any other
in this vast world,
and the best man in the world
would not be capable of substituting
as my father.
You will always be on my mind
and I know you...
Will come back!

[Laura]

For Ramón
June 2004
Havana

Dear dad,

I know how to write and read. Daddy, I love you very much and I want to see you. I hope we can go to see you soon, soon, soon, to give you many kisses.

Daddy, I miss you so much.

A big kiss,

Lizbeth

Gerardo Hernández Nordelo

Adriana Pérez O'Connor

Gerardo and I made plans to have children, but life has put a hold on that dream. We were married on July 15, 1988, and beginning in 1991, we put together an almost complete layette, planning to have our baby when I finished my chemical engineering degree. We still have the baby clothes. We had hoped to have twins, but perhaps in waiting so many years, now that we're older, we'll have to be satisfied with just one. We've talked several times on the telephone about our hope to become parents. We joke about how our children will be and what our lives will be like with one or two little ones in the house.

In general, we talk about this without letting it get to us, but rather using it as a way of keeping in tune with each other, as any married couple might do. Gerardo's sense of humor helps a lot. My sense of reality may give the impression that I am a pessimist, but Gerardo is able to break through that image. He's always joking and this lightens the emotional burden. It's as if each of us protects the other, and in offering me encouragement, he also receives strength and hope. Our dream is intact, which helps to explain why we call each other "my little girl" and "my big boy" and pamper each other as we would do with a child. Although we have a number of nephews and nieces we adore, I'm sure that a child of our own would be very fortunate, very happy. There could not be a more special father for my children than Gerardo.

For Adriana
February 14, 1999
Miami FDC

12E8[8]

There are things that when you have them
make life difficult:
nostalgia, anger, frenzy,
loneliness, pain, reproach,
sadness, hate, bitterness.
And there are things that when you miss them
make life difficult:
a caress, an embrace, tenderness,
rain, dewdrops, gentleness,
meadows, the sea, beauty.

But today, there are two things I am missing
which make life almost impossible to bear:
the sun,
and your smile.

---

1. 12th Floor, East Section, Cell 8 (Miami FDC), where Gerardo spent 17
months in solitary confinement.

For Adriana
March 8, 1999
Miami FDC

Only

Only on days when the sun is shining,
or on rainy mornings,
if the silent tree draws the wind,
or if rain hits the glass.

If I silently call upon your laughter
or if a voice sounds like yours to me,
if time hurts, fast or slow,
and I long for the end of my sorrow.

Only on nights of an endless moon,
if there are thousands of stars for us to watch,
or if I can't count any,
and the sky longs for their presence.

If cold lies in wait for me by my bed,
if even awake I try to dream,
if you don't rest upon my chest,
or if in my dreams I look out over the sea.

Only if I laugh or if I cry,
only if I think of what I was,
only if I know that love exists,
only if I live I think of you.

My queen,
  I just wanted you to know that there are "moments" in which I
think of you and that's why I wrote this poem for you.
  I love you, Gera

For Gerardo
[excerpts]
January 9, 2001
Havana

It's possible that we won't be able to throw a double, as you say, or even a single — there's not enough time for that.

"Throw a double" means to have twins. This was written after the first phone calls, when he told me that if the trial went well we would have the chance to have two children at the same time. He interpreted these words of mine as pessimistic, when all I wanted was to be realistic, to keep him from dreaming too much. I wanted him to know that even if we weren't able to have our children, I wouldn't feel frustrated — I would always love him. I also didn't want to add more suffering to what he was already undergoing. Our first communication was on December 30, 2000, by telephone, after more than two years of silence: no letters, no phone calls, no photos, nothing. All the letters, up to the beginning of June 2001, were written during the trial, and then afterwards, through December, in the anxious days awaiting sentencing. The letters came to me from the Miami FDC. At that point, we were almost certain Gerardo would receive life imprisonment.

For Adriana
[excerpts]
February 3, 2001
Miami FDC

I'm sending you one of the poems I wrote a while ago — this time with a drawing I did. People liked this drawing a lot and I had to redo it for a lot of them. Fortunately, for a time, I was able to make photocopies, and so I only had to color them in. This and other drawings — like several for children that I reproduced — are now scattered over a number of countries because here you find people from all over the place. Since everything here is business, it's not common that somebody does something for free, so people asked me what I wanted for the drawings: soup, chocolate, or whatever else is sold here. But I never charged anyone anything — I only asked them to tell me later if their children liked the drawings, that that would be enough.

When I told you about the drawings for children, I remembered that I had saved one of each, colored in, as a memento. I picked out one to send for you to keep, but I didn't want to send it without writing something on it. Although it's not for you, I know I'm wasting my breath asking you not to read it. I'd like you to keep it, so that one day you can give it to those it's addressed to. (Take note that I haven't given them names, to keep from having to argue about that already.) And please, don't let this get you down, or I'll regret ever sending it to you. About the content: I want you to know that I've not gone nuts over this subject, not by a long shot. It's just that it occurred to me, and I thought it was a nice idea not to leave the drawing without a few lines written alongside it. (Now blow your nose if want…)

Gerardo refers to drawings he made for Ramón's daughter Lizbeth, as well as for children of other prisoners who wrote to their sons or daughters in the space he left beside each drawing. The letter that Gerardo mentions is titled, "Letter for my unborn children." It arrived very quickly — only a few days after he had written it. I wasn't expecting it. René had included it in his diary, which is where I saw it for the first time. I cried a long time. But I didn't let him know how deeply I felt, or how much the letter affected me.

"Letter For My Unborn Children"
February 3, 2001
Miami FDC

My dear children,

By the time you read these lines, a number of years will have passed since they were written — hopefully not too many. At the time of this writing you've not yet been born, and your mother even has doubts about whether you ever will be.

All this is because I'm living some difficult times in my life, far from my country and my family of whom I am so proud, as I hope you will be some day, too.

This is a drawing I've done for many children: sons, daughters, nephews, nieces and other relatives of people who are here with me today. People who have added their words of love to the drawings and then sent them to their loved ones who are also very far away.

This is why I wanted to keep this drawing for you — so that one day, after you come into this world and have learned to read, you can understand why your father is not as young as many of your friends' fathers, so you will know about the many years your mother and father had to live apart, even though they loved each other so much. Years that perhaps one day I'll tell you more about.

I love you very much,
Dad

For Gerardo
[excerpts]
February 14, 2001
Havana

The last part of your letter for our "unborn children" was enough to break one's heart. There can be no doubt about all the love waiting for them, a love that will be an extension of our own feelings for each other. Knowing you so well, I've always felt certain that you would be a wonderful father. All your imagination, creativity, intelligence and human sensitivity make you deserving of the privilege of becoming a father. There's no one better than you to realize this dream, and I'm only glad that you've chosen me to make it come true with you. Perhaps we won't be as young as some, but we'll be better parents than many.

It's difficult not to receive the emotional charge in your words, which is why it was impossible for René not to sense it, too. What he has written about you touched me very deeply. As always, you know how to reach the most intimate part of my being. I don't have to tell you that, and I even wondered whether I should show anyone the letter or keep it to myself.

For Adriana
[excerpts]
February 24, 2001
Miami FDC

I would have liked you to have received the original "my children" letter first rather than seeing it — for the first time — in [René's] diary, because in my letter I explained how the idea came about and what I intended. I didn't write it for everyone to read. Nor did I want you to read it just now, as it wasn't my intention to make anyone sad or make anyone cry.

I'm happy that the people who saw it liked it, but my first interest wasn't "artistic" — rather, it was for my children. So, if you like, keep it to yourself, as you say, and don't make it public.

I also thought that what René wrote about me was very profound. I didn't read it until someone brought me a copy here, so perhaps you read it before I did.

From René's Diary
[undated]
Miami FDC

Yesterday, while I was typing at about this time, I went into Many's (Gerardo's) room to take a break, and he showed me a letter he had written for his unborn children. As I read it, I had to turn my face away so he wouldn't see the moisture in my eyes. I decided I had to close this week's entries in my diary with his letter. This morning I mentioned it to Roberto [René's brother, a lawyer] and again couldn't avoid my face misting over. I know that more than a few people who have read it have shed tears, and I have no doubt that you [Olga, René's wife] would be one of them. I would like to offer this as a reminder of the human quality of this man with whom I have had the opportunity of sharing these difficult moments.

For Gerardo
March 11, 2001
Havana

I love you very much and you know how difficult this has been for me — I don't know how to express it to you, but it doesn't matter, since I know you've felt the same. You were right when you told me to blow my nose when I read the letter that you wrote to your children. But it wasn't the original that made me nostalgic — it was the one in black and white in [René's] diary. The black and white made it so solemn, a complement to your note.

For Adriana
[excerpts]
[undated]
Miami FDC

Do you remember when I used to rock you to sleep, sitting on my lap in the rocking chair? My little girl, it was so hard for me to leave you and it was so tender to watch you asleep in my arms. I remember every detail, like when I used to save a chocolate or a cookie in my pocket to take it home to my spoiled little girl. Have you ever thought of the fact that I raised you? Do you still love me?

For Gerardo
[excerpts]
April 25, 2001
Havana

I still love you, especially because I believe all the beautiful things that you tell me. Is it all still true? Am I still your little girl? So, when you really have one, what will I be then?

I am selfish and it's hard for me to give up my spot. Don't tell me that nothing would change because you won't spoil me the same way when we have our own *children* — and see, it's in the plural! You have to admit that I've changed and now I think of it as something real and with more optimism.

Speaking of children or a child, who told you that the name of the boy is already decided without negotiations?

You're very fresh... See how you know me, that you already warned me that there'll be no discussion of this. You knew I'd protest, or else I wouldn't be myself. Better get used to the idea that if it's a boy, "most probably" he won't be named after you. So you'd better accept this or I'll give up the idea of becoming a mother and making you a father. Okay?

For Adriana
[excerpts]
April 27, 2001
Miami FDC

I know that while we've sacrificed ourselves all this time, there are a lot of people who have made good use of their time, who have been "living the life" these years because that's "the only thing they can take with them," as they say. However, I am not so interested in what I can take with me, but rather in what I'm going to leave behind. Those people "will pass through life without knowing they've lived," as [the poet José Ángel] Buesa would say. But we already have a legacy of self-denial and sacrifice to leave to our children and grand-children, an example and a story to remember, however immodest that may sound.

When we were sweethearts, we never talked about children. It all depended on me finishing my studies. But when I graduated, and we were already married, it was an idea that became very dear to us, and it's all the stronger now. Who would have imagined that we would be so far away from each other? We still had so much of our youth ahead. But now I'm 33 years old. Nevertheless, our most cherished desire is to raise our children as a couple. Together. If that's not possible, then we will still always have each other.

For Adriana
[excerpts]
April 29, 2001
Miami FDC

I wonder, again and again, if my love is so intense that it's "unhealthy," but I can't help it. It must be because, in my case, you are still that same fresh and defenseless 16-year-old girl... Anyway, sometimes I think you are, and will always be, that little girl. And that's why you'll have to put up with my prattle, advice and things like that (it has a good side because when you become an ugly old lady I'll still be calling you "my pretty little doll").

I've always told you that I'd rather have a baby girl first because everyone in the family will spoil her, and so by the time we have a boy they will all be tired and bored and they won't spoil him. Besides, they say girls love their fathers more, and I've spent so much time surrounded only by men that when I get out of prison, all I will want to have are girls around me. If it is a girl, I'll pamper her as much as I do you, so I can see you get jealous when I kiss her and pay more attention to her. I'm a devil, aren't I? Do you think that could possibly happen? I don't know now, but there was a time when that worried you just a little bit. Don't worry, my love. It won't be like that, I promise you. You'll always be my favorite girl. You have my word, in case you ever think I'll need reminding — although I know that won't be necessary. They're going to turn the lights off now, they're late as it is. Good night, my little doll. I love you very much. Kisses.

For Adriana
Miami FDC

The Jingling Cry

The jingling cry
of the keys
mercilessly banishes you
from the kingdom of dreams.
It's of no use that you've chosen
your dearest company
to walk with her
along the shores of the greenest sea,
holding hands and embracing in the spray,
laughing or crying without knowing why,
loving with keen passion,
wanting to hold the moment forever.
No use clutching a wave
or the shadow of her feet upon the sand,
or reaching to keep her in your arms.
The sea will suddenly disappear
taking with it her scent,
the sparkle of her eyes and her laughter, drowning those moments
in memory
when once you were free.
You will find yourself alone again,
with no other choice but to patiently rebuild the path
toward the kingdom of dreams,
threading your way through forebodings and misfortune,
scaling fear and bitterness,
bordering anguish and injustice.
And you will do it,

defying the musical, stabbing harassment
of the keys
that remind you where you are
with their jingling cry.
You will do it,
because you know that in the end she will be there
waiting for you as always beside the sea,
to live today the dream
that tomorrow they will make come true.

For Gerardo
[excerpts]
May 26, 2001
Havana

So, is it really impossible to negotiate a name for the boy? I never
thought to name him one of those names you mention. I was thinking
of using traditional names from our culture, such as Bartolomé, Eus-
taquio, Genaro, Hipólito, Clemente, Filomeno... You can't say they're
not more beautiful than yours, can you?

If it's a girl, is there any difference? Imagine, you would have to
name her Geraldina. Ramón's daughters could have been named
Ramona and Ramoneta instead of Laura and Lizbeth; René's, Renata
and Renela, in honor of their father. Boys are almost always forced
to bear their father's names because of machismo. Anyway, let's
wait until the time comes.

I confess that I knew that at the bottom of your heart you wanted
a girl first. So do I, but I'd like to have two, as you do, and I'd like the
second one to be a boy. However, it would be enough if they were
healthy, intelligent, honest and clever like you and with plenty of
hair like me. Their other qualities will come along by being our

children. The only thing I don't want them to be is disorganized and bad baseball players like you or bad-tempered like me. The rest doesn't matter because they will have what's most important: a lot of love.

For Gerardo
[excerpts]
June 14, 2001
Havana

I've always felt a bit afraid of the love and attention that you'd give our children, but I'd be very proud if you gave them all the love and attention you have given me. I assure you that I wouldn't be jealous, since you have enough love for all of us.

For Adriana
[excerpts]
June 16, 2001
Miami FDC

I'm looking forward to receiving your letters, my little girl. Starting tomorrow, any day now I'll have them. In the last few days, I've been looking over some old papers from the time when we were in the "hole," and there are some notes I made when I read something interesting, thinking one day of sending them to you.

One, for example, talks about the nutrients that are essential for pregnant women, such as DHA (found in salmon, tuna, sardines, eggs and algae); folic acid (in green vegetables, peanuts, liver, grains or tablets); and iron (liver and grains). It also says that you can rely on vitamin supplements, being careful to avoid overdoses because an excess of vitamins such as A, D and E can create problems. And, of course, stay away from caffeine and cigarettes.

So, do you like the name Mariana for the girl? Maybe it's better than Adribell: Adri, for Adriana and Bell for *bella*.[1] That way she would have a part of your name too, which I think isn't at all a bad idea.

The other day I read that sometimes there are earth movements below the ocean that cause giant waves known as tsunami — a Japanese term. I think that if you want your daughter to have an uncommon name (considering the surnames she will have) Sunami wouldn't be bad: it's original and since her mother likes the beach so much... The worst thing is, though, that when you shorten her name, it becomes what? "Suna," "Suni," "Sunamita"... I don't like that last one — sounds like "dynamite." Anyway, we have time to decide our girl's name. I leave you now, *puchucha*,[2] because I want to work out a little. A butterfly kiss and another big kiss. Ciao, I love you.

We always laugh a lot over this one. Imagine Sunami with our surnames: Hernández and Pérez, very common in Cuba.

For Adriana
[excerpts]
September 29, 2001
Miami FDC

I want to tell you something that happened to me — one of those things that happens by chance and leaves you thinking. As I told

---

1. "Beautiful" in Spanish.

2. A term of endearment common in Cuba.

you on September 28, a very important day, we received the much-expected and desired visit from our brothers, José Anselmo López and David Díaz, consul and vice-consul of the Cuban Interests Section in Washington.

They have nine primary school kids at the Interests Section, and two more on the way. They're our diplomats' children. One of them, Ahymed, recently sent us a very nice letter that we answered. During his visit, Anselmo told me that on October 8 three of the children will join the [young Cuban] pioneers, and said that if we wrote something, they would happily read it on the occasion. So, I was appointed to write the card. I got a pen and paper and started thinking what I could do for them. What could I write or draw to express what we wanted? The first thing that came to my mind was Elpidio Valdés (I'm not sure if it's Valdéz in his case). I began to draw a sketch and when I finished, despite the time I hadn't seen him, the result looked a lot like him, I think. But it wasn't quite right. If it had been Woody Woodpecker or Mickey Mouse, the children wouldn't have noticed the difference, but only one person can draw Elpidio Valdés. Then I thought I could tell them that mine was Elpidio Valdés' cousin, but that would have been sacrilege. So I gave up the idea, and ended up drawing several Cuban flags with a nice message in the middle.

Back to Juan Padrón, if you have the opportunity to meet him, and if it's not taking liberties, please tell him that I'd like to have a drawing of Elpidio Valdés made by him to put it in a frame and hang it in my children's and grandchildren's room.

Elpidio Valdés is a character from a cartoon story all Cuban children know. And not only children; we also grew up with his adventures. He is a fictional character, a mambí, a man who fights against the Spanish colonial army and wins all his battles. His creator, Juan Padrón, always makes the stories very funny, and Gerardo enjoyed them a lot, like a child. The coincidence

he refers to has to do with my last letter in which I wrote to him that a rela-
tive of ours had been speaking with Padrón.

For Adriana
[excerpts]
October 26, 2001
Miami FDC

Today is October 26 and it's 10:22 a.m. You know, sometimes I start thinking, when I have a child I'll raise her from the beginning to be in contact with nature and animals. Well, not exactly a Tarzan or anything like that, but I don't want one of those kids who starts screaming the first time they see a goat. I'm going to teach her (because we agreed that the first one will be a girl) to like animals and will try to have at home for her — depending on our living conditions — a guinea pig, a rabbit, a little goat or a little pig... or something like that (if she can't have them all). I told you I have a recurring dream of rabbits and it's always the same: I imagine them going hungry. (Would it be that you are my rabbit?) I think it's my guilt, from the time when it was very hard for me to take care of my rabbits and it was a very hard time for them. Now that I think of it, I remember that when I was very young, at home we had dogs, cats (hidden, because my mom didn't want them), chickens, ducks, turkeys, rabbits, goats, sheep, a horse (for only one day because my dad told me to get rid of it), pigeons, pigs (just for a few days before they hit the frying pan), guinea pigs, turtles, a snake (which one day escaped from its cage with my mother telling me, "I'd better not open a closet and find that giant of a thing one day!"), white mice (Pepe [a neighbor] gave them to me and they bit me and I had to be taken to the clinic where they treat those kind of things), fish, baby birds (they would fall out of the trees and I would raise them until they had feathers and could fly away...), I don't think I'm leaving anything out... oh, yes, quails, I made them a great cage with Iván [a neighbor] but they all died, and guinea fowls. A real zoo! But I never had a parrot, though I was almost about to get one several times. I should have been a vet.

(I forgot the river shrimp, which I had in bowl with a *biajaca*.[1])

Why am I talking so much about animals this morning? I don't know. Must be because I am in love like a dog and I miss my lioness so much and I don't care what I write about. Well, that's it. I'm going to have lunch and then get ahead on my other letter writing. I miss you so much, my little princess. I want so much to mess up your eyebrows with my lips, to hear you say "don't do that..." and then you smooth them again... come on, Father Time!...

For Gerardo
[excerpts]
November 19, 2001
Havana

I think that your idea of raising our children in close contact with nature is excellent, but you'd better start saving gas to take them to Lenin Park, the zoo, the botanical gardens or the aquarium. If we continue living like this, in this house, only Lenin Park will be close enough to visit regularly. But we wouldn't need to raise anything at home, because we have everything there. Aside from a dog, the only thing I'll allow you is a parrot... And if you had become a vet, you wouldn't have had such a volume of letters.

If we live anywhere else, you won't have space for your plans. I like birds, fish and turtles. If we can have any of those — because we have the space, and if you take care of them — then I agree.

Can you imagine if our child inherits that fondness of yours and my brother's for animals! I would suffer a lot with a house full of

---

1. A Cuban freshwater fish.

animals. I don't even want to think about it — but like the saying goes: it never rains, it pours.

For Adriana
[excerpts]
December 25, 2001
Miami FDC

I am fine sweetheart, just a little bit agitated because these past days have been very intense and I haven't had the time to watch a movie or play dominoes. Fernando [González] told me that someone in his cell block told him that he had seen me the day after they sentenced me (it would have been during my attorney's or my mother's visit) and that, instead of seeing me sad or depressed, I looked more active than ever. People here say the same thing, because imagine, every time someone goes to sentencing, and they give them 10 or 15 years, they spend two weeks inside their cells. Whereas despite the life sentences and the years piled on us, we act as if nothing had happened. I tell them that I've always been a person of "faith."

I love you very much, my love. Have a very happy new year, as much as you can, and may the year to come bring us many good things.

For Adriana
[postcard]
December 2001
Miami FDC

That is true my little one, that's why when I first saw this postcard, I saved it to send it to you. I want to thank you for all the things you have had to do lately, which have been many. I want to tell you once again how proud I am of you, for being able to count on you and for that brilliant way in which my little diamond represents me all the time. Thanks again for making me such a happy and lucky man.

Although I will try to send something else later, let this postcard also serve to wish you a very happy and prosperous new year, for you, for the family and for our friends.

...and so that you aren't a spoiled girl, this [the flower] is indeed the most beautiful one.

I love you, my queen,

Gera

For Adriana
[postcard][1]
March 16, 2002
Lompoc USP

Have they explained to you the rules for the visit?

A hug with a little kiss when you come in and a hug with a little kiss when you go out... and that's it!

The rest of the time I will have to content myself, maybe, with...

...your fragrance!
...and your hands on the table!

I really long to see you, my little one, but I think that I am going to suffer a lot with those rules... I am going to have to see the doctor so that he prescribes a pill for me before the visit... (or maybe an electroshock...)

I love you so much,

Gera

---

1. Sent when Gerardo knew that Adriana had secured a visa to travel to the United States.

In July 2002, I received a visa from the U.S. State Department to travel to the United States. However, they held me at the airport in Houston, Texas, for 11 hours. When I set foot on American soil they took away all my documents. Five minutes later, the INS told me that I had no immigration problem, but that the FBI was interested because I was Gerardo's wife. Their interest was strange and illogical because I had never been in the United States and certainly don't represent a danger for such a powerful nation, where it was well known that I was only going to visit an imprisoned man. I was interrogated, they took my fingerprints and they opened a file on me. All of a sudden I found myself facing a dilemma: to return to Cuba immediately or go before an immigration judge, without any guarantees, taking the risk of being deported or even convicted. I couldn't understand it. Nobody could. They have denied me the right to see my husband and to have minimal physical contact with him, the right to have a conversation with him, the chance to tell him, face to face, that I love him.

For Adriana
[postcard]
August 11, 2002
Lompoc USP

No, that was just kidding my little one, we are not going to give that pleasure to these jerks.

So, be brave because I am very proud of you. This is nothing new, but I have to tell you again, because we're a little bit further into the same thing.

I love you,
Gera

For Adriana
[excerpts]
April 9, 2003
Lompoc USP

My little girl,

...I'm writing this letter at work, taking advantage of some free time, because when I get back to the unit I have a lot of things to do. I don't know if this will be a long letter, but the most important thing I have to say is that I love you, and that all the time I spent in the "hole" only made me realize once more how important you are in my life. It's amazing that just thinking of you can change my mood for the better, fill my lungs with oxygen. I thought a lot about us, about our "little nest" and the immense desire I have to be there, alone with you, just the two of us. You are my "amulet," my "talisman," my "lucky charm," and every day I'm more convinced that I cannot live without you. Another important thing I want to tell you is that the more I hear about what happened during our time in solitary, the prouder I am of the support we've received from our people and government, our relatives and the thousands of brothers and sisters worldwide who support us. When you meet anyone from one of the solidarity groups, be sure to express my deepest gratitude, and tell them that sooner or later, we'll win.

I'm healthy, my love, you don't have to worry. I don't want to finish this first page without asking you again to take good care of yourself. Did you get the new vitamin E500? Are you taking any other vitamins? And the folic acid? It is very important for Gerardito's health, whom you need to start caring for right now.

Gerardo has been three times in the "hole." After the first time in solitary confinement in Miami, when he was there 17 months, Gerardo was in isolation for 49 days after the guilty verdict was handed down. But in this letter he refers to the "box" — a crueler version of the "hole." On the eve of the beginning of the appeal process, they had him for a month in his underwear, without contact with family or lawyers, without consular visits, not permitted to write or read. The "box" leaked sewage, and he could not make out whether it was day or night. As in previous confinements, he and the others were subjected to this brutal isolation without cause. There was no indiscipline on their part, and no warning. On the contrary. In Lompoc, Gerardo was threatened with being kept in such conditions for a year, or more.

For Adriana
[postcard]
2003
Lompoc USP

My love,

When my mom gave the pictures of my childhood to *Pionero* magazine, she forgot to include this one. They would have noticed how affectionate and polite I was to girls...

Now, seriously, he looks like me when I was a kid... (the only difference is that, instead of a striped t-shirt, I used to wear a checked shirt...)

I love you so much, my queen.

Today is July 15, so, again, congratulations!

I love you,

Gera

For Adriana
[excerpts]
April 23, 2003
Lompoc USP

My precious doll,

I am again using time from work to write you a letter. This one should arrive close to Mother's Day, so please give my best to everyone: relatives, friends, acquaintances... and please explain to the necessary people that this time when I was sent to the "hole," the guards took the stash of postcards I had kept for the day. Also, this is so you won't complain like you did last year: Happy Mother's Day to you, mom! I already explained to you that I want a daughter first because if Gerardito is born first he is going to be too spoiled from all our attention after waiting so long. So we'd better have a girl first and then a boy. Do you like the name Karen for our girl? Are there many Karens in Cuba? Anyway, congratulations, my queen. I know that you will receive Mother's Day greetings from many, and so mine has to be there, too, since I'm to blame for you being a "virtual mother." Don't worry, the day will come when you'll be a biological mother (although if it doesn't, you should know that having you is all I need to feel fulfilled.)

For Adriana
[postcard]
May 2003
Lompoc USP

My little girl,

There will be always some postcards more beautiful than others, but what never changes is the love that I send with them for you... I congratulate you on this day, on behalf of the "unborn children"

and I send a big kiss feeling more happy and lucky than ever because
my children will have a mother like you.

Congratulations, my love!

I love you,

Gera

For Adriana

[excerpts]

[undated]

Lompoc USP

Let me tell you (and pay attention because this is possibly the most
serious part of the letter) about what you asked on the telephone —
that if I were ever to regret having been at the bus stop that day, waiting for the number 32, or that other day at the beach on 16th Street, or
at the marriage palace on Mayía Rodríguez... it would only be
because one day you yourself had come to regret it, if you had doubts
about whether it was something positive in your life, something you
would do again if you could turn back time, if you doubted that you
would choose to live it again that way. I would regret it only if you
thought that so much suffering and so much "lost time," so much
pain and sacrifice, wasn't worth it. If you thought it would have
been better to follow another path and live life another way, and by
this time have the home, the children, the complete happiness that
you don't have today. If such things cross your mind one day or
even for a moment, if you had the slightest doubt about reliving
everything, then I would indeed regret what happened then. It may
seem contradictory that I say I could regret it, since I've told you
many times that you're the best thing that has happened to me. But
there's no contradiction. Just the opposite, because you're the best
thing that has happened to me, I could never ever wish you anything
but happiness.

We met at a bus stop on Havana's downtown street, La Rampa. I arrived late and my friend and I managed to squeeze into one seat. Gerardo stood next to us and managed to start up a conversation with my friend, who told him we were chemistry students. That day, we didn't exchange a single word, but the following day we ran into each other at the same bus stop. He appeared with verses: "Poem to the Girl at the Bus Stop." He didn't even know my name. On the third day, I left earlier to avoid him. On the fourth day, he showed up very early. We started to spend time together as friends. A while later he invited me to go to the beach in Miramar — very near the institute of international relations, where he graduated as a diplomat. "Look at that boat," he said pointing to the left. Indeed, there was a beautiful yacht on the horizon. "Look at that one," this time pointing to the right. When I turned my head there was a kiss waiting for me. "One boat over there, another over here... and you didn't want to leave Havana Bay," he used to say to me, laughing. Because from then on, the kisses never stopped.

For Adriana
[postcard]
2003
Lompoc USP

My little girl,

Do you remember the first rose I gave you at the bus stop 17 years ago?

We were so young...

For Adriana
October 20, 1986
Havana

Poem to the Girl at the Bus Stop

I can hardly make out the figure before me
bent over, making didactic gestures:
legal concepts and international conflicts,
the details almost make it to my ears.
But my mind is filled with that girl
at the bus stop,
the chemistry student
whose name I do not know,
although I know the shy look on her face,
which day by day magnifies the spell
of the sunrise on La Rampa.
This girl, perhaps tomorrow,
when she sits down on the bus, politely holding my books
    as I stand,
will find that some unknown admirer
of her beauty
paid no attention in class
just to write her this poem.

(Written during an international law class)

For Adriana
[excerpts]
June 1, 2003
Lompoc USP

My little princess,

I'm so affectionate, and I don't feel embarrassed at all!

Are you still as slim as in the picture you sent, where you are signing the booklets? Stay like that, healthy and slender because you are going to gain some weight when you get pregnant... I'm already thinking of our afternoon workouts, we're going to jog around the square. What do you think? When Karen is born, we'll leave her with Vivian, the neighbor, when we go running. Or we can take Gerardito and Karen to your mother's house... So you don't like the name Karen? How about Mariana? Not that either? Gerana...? Gedriana...?

I miss you so much, my darling. You know you are important in my life, but you don't know just how important. Take care of yourself, doll. Are you taking the vitamin E? Is it 500 mg? Don't forget, okay? See how I take care of you? But this is nothing — wait until we're together. You'll end up diabetic, from all the sweet things I'll do for you.

When I think of Gerardo, with his two life sentences, I feel that I have received the same. I'm not only suffering because he is in prison and because of his pain, but also as a wife who cannot have a happy marriage like other women, who cannot have children like them. I often wonder why they don't give me the visa to go to the United States to visit him in prison. Why am I not allowed to see this young man condemned to two life sentences? The only answer possible is that I, too, am a prisoner. I also have two life sentences, or three if we include the one that keeps us from seeing each other even in these terrible circumstances. I am the instrument the U.S. authorities use to pressure Gerardo. This wasn't determined in any courtroom, but the facts speak for themselves.

For Adriana
[excerpts]
June 15, 2003
Lompoc USP

Oof! My chest hurts... My heart is crushed. I'll have to get another ECG. Today is Father's Day and it's also 14 years and 11 months since we got married. (I'd even written you a postcard for the day!) It's 15 years since we signed the first document for the marriage... I don't want to start any new topics in the four lines I have left so I'll use them to tell you how much I love you, and how crazy I am to come home, so you can finally give me a little princess so I can share all this love overflowing in my heart, that is too much for my queen alone...

For Adriana
[excerpts]
June 26, 2003
Lompoc USP

What a coincidence! You letter begins congratulating me for Father's Day. Thank you! Let's hope that among the postcards I received from you today — which I'm not planning to open until the 15th — there comes one for Father's Day...

For Adriana
[postcard]
2003
Lompoc USP

Fifteen years have passed and our hearts remain united like that day!

I love you,

Gera

How lucky is this woman. Man! Look at how much she's received from winning a "lottery prize" 15 years ago... And she's still complaining! Postcards, little hearts, stamps... Take advantage of me because I am nearing 40 and when I reach maturity...

For Adriana
August 11, 2003
Lompoc USP

My love,

We are entering an important stage, my darling. This year has flown by and soon there will be a decision from the Court of Appeals. We have to be more united than ever. I need you more than ever. I need you more than you need me. You are the most important thing in my life. There is no life without you. Every morning when I open my eyes my first thoughts are for you, that you exist, that I have you, that I can count on you and this is what gives me the energy to begin the day. I know I'm obsessed with you ("and the world witnesses my frenzy..."[1]). I know that I overprotect you in some things (all right, in everything). I know I worry too much, but you have to

---

1. A line from the bolero, "Obsession," very popular last century.

understand me, my queen. I don't know what would become of me if something happened to you. I'm 38 and when I look back at my life I can't separate myself from you even in memories. It seems you were with me in kindergarten, in junior high in the countryside, everywhere... (I'm nuts, right?) We have the most important thing, my little girl: we have each other, and we have this immense love that has surpassed every test, and from this point on, we can do anything. We only need a bit more patience, optimism and mostly we need to think of each other and have each other always present. I love you, my queen. You can't imagine how I tremble at the thought of having you in my arms again, kissing your forehead and those eyes that are my undoing. Do you know what the most important project is in my life, the most important reason I must return? The main reason why I would like to live many more years? The main cause I want to dedicate my strength and all my energy to for the rest of my days? It is to make you happy and to be able to compensate for all your suffering, your sacrifices and to return the love you have given me all these years. I want to see you laugh every day, and know that you are happy. That would be the best reward for my efforts. I love you so much — don't ever doubt it. I'm going to sleep. Until tomorrow, then. I love you.

For Gerardo
[excerpts]
October 29, 2003
Havana

Today I was denied a visa for the third time. I can't go to see you. It has been a long time that I have wanted to tell you some things I feel. Sometimes I restrain myself. I know your jailers will read these notes — that our intimacy will pass through their hands. That restrains me, as well as fear of driving hope away. I always expect a miracle

when I request the visa. I hold on to the illusion of a meeting that continues to be delayed. But this endless waiting, these months that go on until they (the U.S. government) give an answer — the word "denied" that finally arrives — all these things. I live with the total conviction that we are victims of a cruel, refined and sinister method of psychological torture. I have so much rage in me that I cannot cry. I don't want to cry.

I'm held together by the happiness I feel when I remember how I met you, and all the small details of our life together. At the same time, Gerardo, I haven't been able to stop dreaming or imagining what this relationship would be like with the children we've not yet been able to have. We've joked, played and even argued about the names of our boy or girl, what we would like to teach them or the surroundings we'd like to raise them in.

I'm sure images of this possible life together have passed through your mind and you've seen, as I have, our daughter's eyes, or the way our boy stands, with my hair and your smile. Sometimes when I sit in a park and a child passes by, I think it could be ours, and my heart fills with tenderness.

I admire Elizabeth and Olguita — women who have raised their children with great effort, without their fathers. I can't stop thinking how Ramón and René feel so far from them and their daughters. I picture myself in a similar situation and I think I wouldn't have had the courage to raise my children alone, imagining how much you would suffer, not being able to share that wonder. No. I cling to the idea that you'll return and will be in the delivery room with me, without passing out, so we can give birth to our children together, and we'll take turns at night when the baby cries. You'll draw and make up stories for them, and will sing the children's songs that I don't know. I'll teach them how to play baseball, because I'll have more spunk than you. I love you, and we will make it through. You'll never leave me alone, because in all these terrible years that you've been so far away, you've never been absent.

Leonard I. Weinglass
The Trial of the Cuban Five

For more than four decades, extreme, right-wing Cubans based in Miami have launched attacks against Cuba, resulting in many deaths, many more injuries, and millions of dollars in property loss. Instead of being prosecuted for terrorist activities, they have enjoyed either the active help or willful blindness of the U.S. government.

In the early 1990s, as Cuba was beginning to recover from the impact of the collapse of the Soviet Union by marketing itself as a tourist destination, these exiles focused their attacks on airline terminals, hotel buses and beachfront hotels. Airports and marinas in southern Florida were repeatedly used to launch attacks against such targets. In one such attack, shells were fired from a boat offshore at a beachfront Cuban hotel. In another, a bomb planted in the famous Copacabana Hotel exploded, killing an Italian tourist.

Repeated diplomatic protests to the United States and the United Nations fell on deaf ears as Cuba's enemies eagerly awaited the collapse of the Cuban Revolution.

That was when five Cuban men, later known as the Cuban Five, whose collective writings appear in this book, came forward in defense of their country. They traveled to the United States, not with weapons or explosives, but with courage and wit, to infiltrate the extremist groups operating out of southern Florida in order to warn the Cuban authorities of impending terrorist plans and activities. They succeeded in their mission. The material they gathered was made part of a lengthy report turned over by the Cuban government to FBI agents, who were invited to Havana to receive four volumes of information, including names and places (and highlighting the fact that there were military training camps in southern Florida). The Cuban authorities asked the FBI to take appropriate steps to halt the ongoing transgressions of international as well as domestic U.S. law. When the U.S. government failed to act, copies of what was turned over to the FBI were given to the *New York Times*. None of it was published.

When the U.S. government did act, it was not to prosecute the perpetrators of the violence, many with close connections to persons within the political, military and intelligence establishments in the United States, but those who had documented their activities: the Cuban Five. In September 1998 they were charged with the inchoate crime of conspiracy to commit espionage and other lesser crimes. By charging a "conspiracy" the government was relieved of its obligation to prove that the crime of espionage had actually occurred. All it had to do was to persuade a Miami jury of an amorphous "agreement" between the defendants to commit espionage at some unspecified time in the future. Indeed, shortly after their arrest, the U.S. government acknowledged in a press release that "there are no indications that they had access to classified documents or access to sensitive areas," thereby assuring the public that national security was "never compromised."

Realizing the weakness of the case, and under increasing pressure from the exile community in Miami to indict Cuban President Fidel Castro, the U.S. government amended the charges seven months after their arrest to include a more serious conspiracy: conspiracy to commit murder. Gerardo Hernández, one of the Five, was so charged because he had infiltrated Brothers to the Rescue, whose members died when their planes were shot down by the Cuban air force as they attempted to fly over Cuba in February 1996.

Before their case was brought to trial, the Five spent 17 months in isolation cells ordinarily used to punish sentenced criminals who misbehave in prison. The government also limited their lawyers' ability to adequately prepare a defense by imposing security procedures restricting their access to the evidence.

The fate of the Five was sealed long before the trial began when the judge refused to move the case out of Miami so that a jury could be selected from a community not so inflamed by hostility against Cuba. A trial should be moved once it is shown that community bias renders a fair proceeding unlikely. Polling data drawn from Miami residents, which included over half a million exiles from Cuba and their families, established an overwhelming bias there against the Five, precluding any possibility of a fair trial. Nonetheless, their modest and reasonable request to move the case just 25 miles up the freeway to Fort Lauderdale was denied, forcing them to defend themselves in an atmosphere which, in the words of a leading expert on Miami attitudes toward Cuba, reduced the chances of a fair trial to "zero."

The trial lasted nearly seven months — then the longest criminal proceeding in the United States. Over 70 witnesses testified for both sides, with the defense calling two U.S. generals, an admiral and a presidential advisor, among others, who supported their contention that no conspiracy existed to violate the laws of the United States. Thousands of pages were introduced into evidence, including many of the reports sent by the defendants to Cuba assessing the dangers posed by the groups they infiltrated and warning of pending attacks. The defense even subpoenaed some exile leaders of the counterrevolution who were compelled to confess to their own violent actions against Cuba. Despite all this compelling evidence for the defense, the jury quickly convicted all five on all the 26 charges of which they stood accused.

Equally predictable were the maximum sentences handed out to each of the defendants on each charge for which they were convicted: Gerardo Hernández received two life sentences plus 15 years; Ramón Labañino received a life sentence plus 18 years; Antonio Guerrero was also given a life sentence plus 10 years; Fernando González was sentenced to 19 years; and René González to 15 years. Immediately following their sentencing they were separated into various prisons as far removed from each other as possible: one in Texas, one in California, one in Colorado, one in Wisconsin and one in South Carolina.

Just as their cases were being readied for appeal in March 2003, all five were summarily cast into isolation punishment cells reserved for the most violent and incorrigible inmates, "on orders from Washington," according to the local prison administrators who were perplexed by this directive since all had been behaving in an exemplary fashion. It was only after worldwide protests, including those from the U.S. congress objecting to this unjustified action, that they were restored to their regular status.

As of this writing their cases are under appeal before the 11th Circuit Court of Appeals of Atlanta. The decision will either mark this case as yet another chapter in a long record of injustice toward Cuba, or, hopefully, a sharp and necessary break with that shameful past.

Leonard I. Weinglass
Attorney for Antonio Guerrero
2004

Resources

Addresses for the Cuban Five

René González Sehwerert
Reg. #58738-004
FCI Marianna
PO Box 7007
Marianna, FL 32447-7007
USA

Antonio Guerrero Rodríguez
Reg. #58741-004
USP Florence
PO Box 7500
Florence, CO 81226
USA

Fernando González Llort
c/- Rubén Campa
Reg. #58733-004
FCI Oxford
PO Box 1000
Oxford, WI 53952-0505
USA

Ramón Labaniño Salazar
c/- Luis Medina
Reg. #58734-004
USP Beaumont
PO Box 26030
Beaumont, TX 77720-6035
USA

Gerardo Hernández Nordelo
Reg. #58739-004
USP Victorville
PO Box 5500
Adelanto, CA 92301
USA

Websites

http://www.freethefive.org

http://www.granma.cubaweb.cu/miami5/index.html

http://www.freethecubanfive.ca

http://www.antiterroristas.cu

WARS OF THE 21ST CENTURY
New Threats, New Fears
Ignacio Ramonet

An activist intellectual like Noam Chomsky, Ignacio Ramonet is the internationally recognized and respected editor of the prestigious *Le Monde diplomatique*. For the first time this articulate and radical voice is presented to English-language readers, discussing the fundamental global issues at stake in the recent wars in Iraq, Afghanistan, Kosovo and elsewhere.

ISBN 1-876175-96-6

LATIN AMERICA
From Colonization to Globalization
Noam Chomsky in conversation with Heinz Dieterich

An indispensable book for those interested in Latin America and the politics and history of the region. As Latin America hovers on the brink of a major social and economic crisis, internationally acclaimed philosopher, scholar and political activist Noam Chomsky discusses some of the principal political events in recent years.

ISBN 1-876175-13-3

CENTURY OF TERROR IN LATIN AMERICA
A Chronicle of U.S. Crimes Against Humanity
Luis Suárez

From the Monroe Doctrine through the "dirty wars" in Cuba and Central America, and the neoliberal agenda being imposed with such explosive consequences today, this is a comprehensive history of U.S. intervention in Latin America.

ISBN 1-876175-41-9

GUANTÁNAMO
A Critical History of the U.S. Naval Base in Cuba

A comprehensive analysis of the controversial U.S. base in Cuba. Updated with a new essay exposing the illegality of the naval base in international law.

ISBN 1-920888-04-7

COVERT ACTION
The Roots of Terrorism
Edited by Ellen Ray and William H. Schaap

"The essays in this collection could hardly be more timely, or more informative, and cannot be ignored by those who hope to gain a serious understanding of what is unfolding today." —Noam Chomsky

With an introduction written during the war on Iraq, this book brings together a selection of key articles from the authoritative magazine *CovertAction*, presenting a comprehensive background to the terrorist attacks of September 11, 2001, and the current "war on terror."

ISBN 1-876175-84-2

BIOTERROR
Manufacturing Wars the American Way
Edited by Ellen Ray and William H. Schaap

While Washington contemplates pre-emptive strikes against those nations unilaterally identified as the "axis of evil" and said to be stockpiling weapons of mass destruction, this controversial, well-documented book proves that the United States itself has been a notorious practitioner of chemical and biological warfare.

ISBN 1-876175-64-8

CHILE: THE OTHER SEPTEMBER 11
An Anthology of Reflections on the 1973 Coup in Chile
Edited by Pilar Aguilera and Ricardo Fredes

Contributions by Ariel Dorfman, Salvador Allende, Pablo Neruda, Víctor and Joan Jara, Beatriz Allende, Fidel Castro and others.

ISBN 1-876175-50-8

DEADLY DECEITS
My 25 Years in the CIA
Ralph W. McGehee

A classic account of the CIA's deeds and deceptions by one of its formerly most-prized recruits.

ISBN 1-876175-19-2

SACCO & VANZETTI
Edited by John Davis

An illuminating example of how immigrants, anarchists and communists were the "terrorists" of yesteryear, Nicola Sacco and Bartolomeo Vanzetti were convicted in a trial steeped in racial and ideological prejudice. Their case sparked an unprecedented defense campaign and became a symbol of the international struggle for justice, equality and liberty. Published as part of the Rebel Lives series.

ISBN 1-876175-85-0

POLITICS ON TRIAL
Five Famous Trials of the 20th Century
William Kunstler

Introduction by Karin Kunstler Goldman, Michael Ratner & Michael Steven Smith

Cases analyzed by U.S. radical lawyer William Kunstler include the Rosenbergs, Sacco & Vanzetti and the Scottsboro Nine. The introduction highlights current-day threats to political rights in light of the USA Patriot Act and the "war on terror."

ISBN 1-876175-49-4

THE EMERGING POLICE STATE
William Kunstler

Edited by Michael Steven Smith, Karin Kunstler Goldman & Sarah Kunstler

The defiance, anger and optimism of "America's most celebrated and most detested" radical lawyer ring throughout this selection of his unpublished speeches.
ISBN 1-876175-79-6

WHAT EVERY RADICAL NEEDS TO KNOW ABOUT STATE REPRESSION
A Guide for Activists
Victor Serge
Introduction by Dalia Hashad

Serge's exposé of the surveillance and harassment of political activists by the Czarist police reads like a spy thriller. But as Dalia Hashad describes in her introduction, this book resonates against a new wave of repression and racial profiling post-September 11.

ISBN 1-920888-17-9

CIA TARGETS FIDEL
The Secret Assassination Report
Introduction by Fabián Escalante
Presents the internal CIA report prepared in 1967 on its own plots to assassinate Cuban President Fidel Castro.
ISBN 1-875284-90-7

THE BAY OF PIGS AND THE CIA
Cuban Secret Files Reveal the Story Behind the Invasion
Edited by Juan Carlos Rodríguez
Cuba's story of the 1961 Bay of Pigs mercenary invasion, and its aftermath, means that no CIA document or other account can be read in the same way.
ISBN 1-875284-98-2

PSYWAR ON CUBA
The Declassified History of U.S. Anti-Castro Propaganda
Jon Elliston
Secret CIA and U.S. government documents are published here for the first time, showing a 40-year campaign by Washington to use psychological warfare and propaganda to destabilize Cuba.
ISBN 1-876175-09-5

CUBA AND THE UNITED STATES
A Chronological History
Jane Franklin
Relates in detail developments involving the two neighboring countries from the 1959 revolution through 1995.
ISBN 1-875284-92-3

CUBAN REVOLUTION READER
A Documentary History
Edited by Julio García Luís
This new, expanded edition covering 45 years of the Cuban Revolution presents a comprehensive overview of key events in Cuba, the revolution's impact in Latin America and Africa, and relations with the United States.
ISBN 1-920888-05-5

THE CUBA PROJECT
CIA Covert Operations 1959-62
Fabián Escalante

"Fabián Escalante is in a unique position to add significant insight and information about this crucial chapter of modern history. His review of CIA covert operations against Cuba is to be greatly welcomed, and should be widely read — and pondered." —Noam Chomsky

ISBN 1-876175-99-0

THE CUBAN EXILE MOVEMENT
Dissidents or Mercenaries?
Hernando Calvo and Katlijn Declercq

The first major exposé of the extremist Cuban exile groups in the United States. Thoroughly researched, this book investigates the links between prominent Cuban exile groups and the CIA, and their involvement in terrorist activities against Cuba.

ISBN 1-876175-15-X

WASHINGTON ON TRIAL
Introduction by Michael Ratner and David Deutschmann

Cuba's $181 billion claim against the U.S. government for war crimes.

ISBN 1-876175-23-0

HAVANA-MIAMI
The U.S.-Cuba Migration Conflict
Jesús Arboleya

Examines the origins of the migration conflict and how and why it has become such a crucial issue in U.S. domestic politics.

ISBN 1-875284-91-5

oceanpress

e-mail info@oceanbooks.com.au
www.oceanbooks.com.au